ABOUT THE

Alex Quick lives and writes in ￼ ... ￼ ... he tries (not always successfully) to follow his own advice.

102
FREE
THINGS
TO DO

Inspiring Ideas
for a Better Life

Alex Quick

First published in 2009 by Old Street Publishing Ltd,
40 Bowling Green Lane, London EC1R 0NE
www.oldstreetpublishing.co.uk

ISBN 978 1 906964 17 7

Copyright © Alex Quick, 2009

The right of Alex Quick to be identified as the author of this work has been asserted by him in
accordance with the Copyright, Designs and Patents Act 1988.

Every effort has been made obtain permission for all illustrations, but in the event of an
omission the publisher should be contacted.

All rights reserved. No part of this publication may be reproduced, stored in or introduced into
a retrieval system, or transmitted, in any form, or by any means (electronic, mechanical,
photocopying, recording or otherwise) without the prior written permission of the publisher.

10 9 8 7 6 5 4

A CIP catalogue record for this title is available from the British Library.

Page Design by Hugh Adams
Printed and bound in Great Britain

Dedicated to
Clement Dexter

1

Go out and look at the stars

JUST BY LOOKING UP at the night sky you can see objects that are a hundred times as big as the sun. You can see, across quintillions of miles, stars in the process of colliding, exploding, or being born out of dust. And the light you see, in the case of the furthest stars, was emitted before mankind even existed.

Is it conceivable anyone would want to stay indoors while all this was going on?

You don't need a telescope. With your own naked eye you can get to know the colours, sizes and personalities of the stars; you can explore the trail of gas and stars at the edge of our galaxy that we call the Milky Way; see other galaxies such as Andromeda or the Large Magellanic Cloud; track the movements of the planets; and spot comets, asteroids, meteors, and our own man-made star, the International Space Station. It's even possible for amateurs to make a contribution to space science – a large proportion of all supernovae (massively-exploding stars) are discovered by amateurs.

Light pollution is a problem in towns and cities, but there are still great swathes of darkness away from urban centres. The truly dark places make for spectacular viewing.

Gazing at the stars is a humbling but also exhilarating experience. And it's free!

explore the Milky Way.

2

Keep a diary – but only one sentence a day

MANY PEOPLE KEEP LONG and detailed diaries, and some famous people even publish them. Tony Benn has published his diaries in several volumes, beginning in the 1940s – which means he is now writing his diary knowing it will eventually be published. (Tony, this is not a diary, this is autobiography.)

The diary is a rather daunting commitment, requiring you to set aside a part of your day, every day, to detail what has happened to you and what it all means. Because of this it is difficult to keep up.

But what about a diary that is not a chore at all? That is over almost before it has begun? That is fun?

This is the one-sentence diary.

Writing one sentence a day is a simple way to reflect on the current state of your life. It is brief, concentrated, self-contained. It can record a single major event, an insight, a plan. Or none of these. If you open the diary and your mind is a blank, you can just write 'My mind is a blank,' and snap it shut.

way to reflect on the current state of your life.

More likely you will find that the removal of the obligation to 'keep a diary' will allow you the freedom to write something truly meaningful.

This is the one-sentence diary.

3

Meter your energy use with a smart meter

A SMART METER is a portable device, about as big as an alarm clock, that runs on batteries and can be placed anywhere around the home. It has a readout showing exactly how much electrical energy is being consumed throughout the house at any one time. The readout can be set to show the number of kilowatts used per minute, hour, day, year and so on, or alternatively how much your electricity usage is costing in money or contributing to carbon dioxide emissions (per minute, hour, day, year, etc.). By turning various devices off and on – such as light bulbs, heaters or kettles– you can see in real time how much energy you are consuming, and adjust your devices – and your expenditure – accordingly.

Smart meters are not free, but the new parsimony you develop will certainly cover the cost several times over.

You can see in real time how much energy you are consuming

Give up your car

FOR MANY PEOPLE, giving up their car is impractical – they need it to commute to work. Or they live in the country where there is no reliable public transport.

But for others, who only make short journeys, and who live and work in towns, giving up their car might make a lot of sense.

Consider: a car costs about £700 a year in road tax, insurance, government checks, repairs, maintenance, parking permits and parking tickets. This is without the cost of fuel, or, indeed, the cost of the car. Why not consider the alternatives?

For example: you can cycle. You can join a car club and pay for the car only when you need it. You can car-share or car-pool. You can go places by taxi (£700 plus the cost of a car and fuel will buy a lot of taxi rides). You can go by public transport. You can do a combination of all or any of these.

In Kurt Vonnegut's novel *Breakfast of Champions*, alien beings look down on our planet and try to determine its dominant life-form. Eventually they decide it must be the car.

5

Get up earlier

IT IS GENERALLY AGREED that six to eight hours sleep out of the twenty-four is about right. Let's call it seven hours on average.

But which seven?

If you go to bed late, say at midnight, your seven hours will mean you get up at seven o'clock. This will mean, if you have to go to work, that you have just enough time to get dressed, shaved, etc., before you leave the house; if you have children you will have just enough time to get the children up and out of the door.

is about right.

But what about going to bed earlier and getting up earlier?

A bedtime at 10.30 means rising at 5.30 – or, if you need less sleep, even earlier.

Getting up earlier brings definite benefits. After waking and dressing you have an appreciable amount of time to yourself before you need do anything at all. This is not, as evenings tend to be, time filled with TV, alcohol and computers, but time filled with an unearthly quiet. At 5.30 a.m. the world is very still, even in town. You can use the time to meditate, to watch the sun rise, to go for a walk, to write something in your one-sentence diary, to read a chapter of a book, to do some uninterrupted work with a clear head, or to check on your sunflowers. When the working day starts you will feel calm, relaxed, prepared, and energized.

you will feel calm, relaxed and energized.

Sketch your relatives – it's better than photos

Photos are fine but a portrait reveals two souls – the model's and the artist's.

A photograph is an object mediated by a camera. While photos can be very evocative, they can never achieve the immediacy, the humanity, of a drawing or painting.

Most photographs are not 'art'; and yet the meanest sketch is 'art'. A sketch is an exploration.

Most people who draw portraits agree that it is best not to work from photos. If you do, what you will get is really nothing more than a copy of a photo. Draw from life and your work has to be fast and spontaneous. This is

A sketch is an exploration.

more likely to catch something of the essence of the person. If you are lucky or persistent, it could be something extraordinary.

If your drawing/sketching skills are not everything they could be, and stick-men are your limit, *Drawing on the Right Side of the Brain* by Betty Edwards is highly recommended. In it she shows how a person can dramatically improve their skills by letting the intuitive side of the brain take over.

your work has to be fast and spontaneous.

7

The body is

Treasure your precious human body

'PRECIOUS HUMAN BODY' is a concept in Tibetan Buddhism. It draws attention to the marvel of the temporary and fallible bodily vehicle we inhabit.

We live in a paradoxical world. Western society is very body-conscious, and yet the body is remarkably unappreciated. No-one goes up to their friends and says, 'I hear you have great liver function,' or 'Nice spleen.'

We compound our ignorance and lack of appreciation with an active hostility to our own bodies. We abuse our bodies because it is easy. We take drugs. We fail to stay fit. We eat the wrong things.

Of course, this weakness is human.

But perhaps, whenever we have a dark moment and think 'what's the point of exercising?' or 'I could do with cigarette' we might find it useful to remember:

Precious Human Body.

remarkably unappreciated.

8

Go on an archaeological dig

THE GOOD THING ABOUT archaeological digs is that the people who run them are always desperate for free labour. This sets them apart from other scientists – such as the ones who sequence genes or run particle accelerators.

Archaeology is also unlike other sciences in that it tends to involve whole communities. It is often a public activity, conducted in the midst of life. There are even digs with activities for children.

The best way to get involved is probably to contact your local university: most university archaeology departments have programmes that welcome volunteers. Or go to the library or look online, where entire archaeological holidays are available.

to involve whole communities.

You will normally have to find the funds to travel to the site and pay for your own sustenance and accommodation while you are there – but you'd have to do that if you stayed at home.

Archaeological volunteers were present at the unearthing of the longship at Sutton Hoo; at the exploration of the lower levels of the Coliseum in Rome; and at the uncovering of the ruins of Chichen Itza in Mexico. It's hard to think of another science where unskilled enthusiasts are present at the moment when our knowledge of the world is enlarged.

with activities for children.

9

Write a letter
to your future self

Dear Future Self,

I sit here today obscurely troubled. I have problems at work, the children are a constant source of worry, I am fat and unfit, and I am getting older by the minute.

Can't you at least try, for my sake, to make the effort to change? Will you always be dominated by nagging worries, will you always be dissatisfied, prone to mood swings, unhappy with your appearance, your relationship's and your career?

Come on, get your finger out. I'm relying on you. Don't let me down.

Yours sincerely,

Your Past Self

would crystallize your worldview at a particular point in your life.

That is one way of doing it, though possibly not the best.

The best sort of letter to your future self would probably be more serious. It would crystallize your worldview at a particular point in your life. It would sum up what you have learned at that point, and what you perceive to be 'wisdom' – offered in all humility. When you open your letter 10 or 15 years from the time of writing you will not be in the mood for a joke. You will wish for a real communion with your past self, to remember how things were. Perhaps you will be going through a time of trial and will wish for advice. You will see naiveté and innocence in what you have written, but also things you have forgotten and would do well to remember.

A letter to your future self is a good way to take stock, to focus on what is really important, and to take courage in your journey through life.

10

Don't confuse affluence with well-being

THE DEFINITION OF AFFLUENCE? Wealth, easy availability of modern consumer goods, good social welfare provision – in general, the condition referred to as a 'high standard of living'.

The definition of well-being? Feeling happy and comfortable in one's own skin, enjoying good relationships and being interested in life.

The two do not necessarily overlap.

In fact the proponents of the theory of 'affluenza' (a telescoping of the words 'affluence' and 'influenza') argue that affluence – considered in its purely material aspects – may have negative consequences. Pursuit of affluence, they argue, and the valuation of material goods over psychological and spiritual goods, can lead to stress, waste, guilt, mental illness, debt, unhappiness and despair.

Another way of looking at it is to ask whether we, as a society, are any happier now than we were in the 1950s (when the level of affluence was considerably lower). Or whether we are happier than people in other countries which are much less affluent than ours. If the answer to either of these questions is 'no', then there may be a problem.

When you have to make a decision, particularly on lifestyle or financial matters, why not take some time to ask yourself this: how is your decision likely to affect a) your affluence and b) your well-being?

Pursuit of affluence can lead to stress, waste, guilt, mental illness, debt, unhappiness and despair.

11

Memorize a poem

GOOD POETRY touches us by marshalling techniques that would look absurdly decorative in prose. These techniques – rhythm, rhyme, metaphor, assonance – somehow communicate with us in a way that prose never could.

To memorize a poem is to internalize this decoration, this architecture. It is like taking a beautiful building, dismantling it and re-installing it, brick by brick, in our minds. When the operation is finished we carry the building with us. We can gaze on it any time we like.

Good poetry communicates
with us in a way
that prose never could.

12

Ask a child for advice

THIS IS SOMETHING that people rarely do.

You often hear adults asking questions as if they're asking for a child's opinion, but in reality they're seeking to guide them toward a conclusion they've already decided on. For example, they might ask: 'Why do you think Timmy hit you?' (hoping to elicit the response: 'Because I was poking him with a stick.'). This is not a request for information: this is a disguised attempt to guide and educate (in the most well-meaning way, of course). Children soon get to understand this and feel that they're being patronized.

Children live lives which are largely devoid of power. At first, this is entirely appropriate: they should probably experience Brussels sprouts at least once. But shouldn't they gradually be allowed to take more responsibility?

Try it: ask for advice from a child, listen to it, and then incorporate it into your decision. The child will feel very empowered, you'll strengthen your relationship with them, and you'll usually get a new perspective on your problem.

13

Take part in a police line-up

THIS IS FASCINATING and completely free. In fact, you get paid for it.

The simplest way to try it is to go to your local police station and register as a potential line-up candidate. They'll take your details, including a description of your personal appearance, and when they need someone fitting your description they'll contact you. Of course, the nature of human criminality means that if you are a man aged between 18 and 35 you are likely to be in greater demand than, say, a woman of 80.

It's intriguing and odd to be in a room with nine other people who are all, in some sense, supposed to look like you. When the real suspect is brought into the line-up there is a perceptible freezing of the blood: perhaps, in a different life, you could be him and he could be you.

By the way, if you get chosen instead of the suspect, they can't put you in prison.

14

Give up craving for recognition (and be admired for it)

EVERY TIME I tell somebody something I've done and want recognition for, I feel obscurely ashamed. I try to rationalize it by saying to myself, 'Well, if I don't tell them, who will?' but the feeling won't go away. What causes it? It must be that I'm ashamed to need recognition so badly. I obviously can't feel good till I get it. I am dependent on it, even if it brings a degree of shame along with it.

If I am dependent on the praise and good opinion of others, I am putting myself dangerously in their pockets. Can't I just *be*? Do I have to be *something*?

If you give up making a show of your achievements, the first thing that happens is that the feeling of shame associated with bragging goes away. The second thing is that you feel stronger for not having given in to your 'need'. The third thing is that people immediately begin reacting more positively to you. Bragging, in the end, doesn't really exalt you in other people's eyes. They see your 'need'. So it's counterproductive.

15

Notice when things have improved

IT'S OFTEN SAID that 'technology may improve, but morality does not.' This is untrue, surely.

Fifty years ago, racism in western societies was much more common and acceptable. Disabled people had fewer opportunities. Women were expected to be housewives and mothers, and were not expected to have careers. Bullying in schools (sometimes by the teachers) went unchecked.

Then there are the improvements that are largely a matter of technology. Fifty years ago many cancers were incurable that are now treatable. There was more air pollution. Car crashes were more likely to be fatal. International phone calls were difficult. The food in restaurants was terrible. And so on.

we persist in thinking that human beings can't really

All of these things have improved. And yet we persist in thinking that human beings can't really learn to live together, that we are just selfish, aggressive animals whose real nature is always to exploit and harm one another. Why we should persist in thinking this is mysterious.

Of course, there are still plenty of problems in the world, and some things have got worse. But why focus exclusively on them?

learn to live together.

16

Go on holiday without leaving your bedroom

IN HIS BRILLIANT BOOK, *Sod Abroad*, Michael Moran argues that going on holiday is a waste of time and money, that travel is eroding the planet, and that whatever you can find abroad you can find at home, only much better. While most of this is almost certainly untrue, the elements of truth that it contains are perhaps sufficient to justify spending your holiday in your bedroom.

This is not a free activity, but it is cheaper than actually going on holiday, and the difference will leave you better off.

holiday, and the difference will leave you better off.

Step 1: Buy some posters depicting scenes from your preferred holiday destination: Machu Picchu, Prague, Venice, or wherever you fancy. Plaster the walls of your bedroom with them.

Step 2: Purchase the delicacies of the country in question. On holiday you would have spent much of your time eating and drinking (in expensive restaurants), so this will re-create the most significant activity of your proposed trip.

Step 3: Install a café or restaurant table and seating so that you can consume this food and drink while surrounded by scenes of your favoured destination.

Step 4: Bring your refrigerator into your bedroom and stock it up with minibar items such as miniature bottles of spirits, cans of lager, chocolate bars, etc., to simulate your hotel room.

Step 5: Move a television and DVD player into your room (if you don't already have one); get some films from the country of your choice, preferably without subtitles, and watch them disconsolately, wishing there were some English programmes on.

17

Practice random acts of kindness (and, if time permits, senseless acts of beauty)

THE BOOKS NOW DEVOTED to this philosophy might fill a small shelf. There are *Random Acts Of Kindness: 365 Ways To Make The World A Better Place* by Danny Wallace; *Dilbert: Random Acts Of Management* by Scott Adams, and even *Random Acts Of Malice* by Sharon Grehan. Some of these acts may be a little impractical ('give a policeman a helium balloon' – where is he supposed to keep it afterwards?). But the general idea is to be nicer to people, because, generally, they appreciate it, it lifts their day and it makes connections that enrich everybody's lives.

One of my favourite such 'acts' is to leave post-it notes with positive or amusing messages on the underground, inside library books, in shops, etc. (this is not defacing library books, folks!) Here are a few that I like:

The general idea is to be nicer to people.

'Success is going from failure to failure with no loss of enthusiasm.'
– Winston Churchill.

'The only difference between saints and sinners is that every saint has a past while every sinner has a future.'
– Oscar Wilde.

'The day after tomorrow is the third day of the rest of your life.'
– George Carlin.

18

Climb a mountain

It is one of the most

Climbing a mountain, a real mountain, is one of the most thrilling things you can do – and it is entirely free. All you need is legs.

Having said that, climbing a mountain is also a feat of endurance, and may be painful, dangerous, even tedious. It takes a long time to climb any mountain over about 3,000 metres, and it may have to be done in more than one stage.

Why is it a good idea to do something that is painful, dangerous and tedious? Because if we press on with it despite difficulties – boulders, rain, snows – until we reach the summit, it is only then, looking down from the peak, high above the clouds, that we sense our power, our capacity for endurance, and feel life surging fully within us. Or as Friedrich Nietzsche, himself an avid mountain-climber, put it:

'The ice is near, the solitude is immense – but how calm lies everything in the light! How free one breathes! . . . Philosophy, as I have until now understood and lived it, is the voluntary life in ice and high mountains. . .'

thrilling things you can do.

HEIDI

19

Turn your house into a restaurant

This is an activity with a whiff of the subversive: it's sometimes called 'guerrilla dining'.

The idea is simple. Set up several tables in the biggest room you've got. Make several large dishes — or get someone in to cook for you. Levy a small charge per person to cover costs. Ask your guests to bring their own drinks.

what you end up with

not unlike your

What you end up with is a noisy, cramped affair not unlike your favourite intimate restaurant – with the difference that the diners are all your friends. By the end of the evening you've either broken even or made a small profit. To entice guests you can say that any profits will be donated to charity. It's not about money anyway, but about having a good time and eating good food.

It's possible to take the idea even further by hosting dinner parties on beaches, bridges, rooftops, parks, galleries and. . . anywhere else. Guests are alerted by SMS or email just before the event, as if it were all highly illegal. Which, if it's held on a bridge, it probably is.

is a noisy cramped affair

favourite intimate restaurant.

20

there is something primal about

in front of

Start a film society

AT A TIME in which the range of movies available to watch in the privacy of our own homes is ever greater, where TV screens are ever larger, where movies can be downloaded at will, why do people still bother to go to the cinema?

The answer seems to be that there is something primal about sitting with a hundred other people in darkness in front of a screen as big as a house.

sitting with a hundred other people in darkness a screen as big as a house.

A film society is somewhere between the home-entertainment option and the full-blown cinematic experience. On the one hand, you, as a society member, get to choose which films to see, as you would at home. It could be a whole season of Mexican slasher movies, or back-to-back Ingmar Bergman, to taste. On the other, you get the excitement of the cinema, the hush, the sense of occasion, the wide screen, the surround sound.

Equipment and premises can be hired; most film societies are non-profit and run by their members. And if you start one, you become the president, and you get to see
all the films for free!

21

Remember that making mistakes is part of being human

HERE IS AN EXAMPLE of an ordinary social blunder. A man and his wife are walking slowly along a path, and the man vaguely notices someone behind them. He says to his wife, 'Let this guy pass.' But it isn't a guy, it's a young woman he mistook for a guy. The young woman hears what he says and shoots him a dirty look. The man feels terrible. He immediately wants to say something to make amends. But the words won't come. The moment passes and nothing is said. He goes home and continues feeling terrible for several hours.

When something like this happens, it's important to remember that we will always do things like this because we are human. It is human to make mistakes. No power on earth will stop us. In a sense, it is not our fault. We are all idiots from the cradle.

This also applies to most things that other people do to you that at the time seem less than polite, less than considerate, or less than fair. They are innocent, innocent! No-one derives any permanent benefit from deliberately demeaning or insulting others, and often it is through a genuine mistake, social awkwardness or just because they are feeling bad that day.

There is innocence within. You are good – good not in the moral sense but in the sense that an apple or a child's expression is good.

There is innocence within. You are good.

22

See the sun rise and set on a single summer's day

The sun, as astronomers know, is a huge exploding ball of hydrogen and helium. It's so big that the earth could fit into it more than a million times, and it's about seven hundred times as massive as all the rest of the solar system – Jupiter, Saturn, Uranus, Neptune, Earth, Mars, Venus, Mercury, Pluto and all the asteroids, comets and other debris – put together. It supports nearly all life on earth and its radiation creates our weather. It seems silly to ignore it.

Worship of the sun must have been the first religion. It is, in a sense, the most natural and obvious religion. The sun is the conspicuous bringer of everything that is good. The Aztecs and the Mayans knew this, and they made quite a thing of it, to the detriment of their enemies.

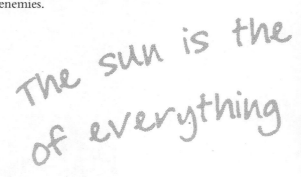
The sun is the of everything

To see the sun rise and set in a single summer's day is a form of prayer that everyone, religious or non-religious, can participate in. As the sun returns and departs it marks another day, and invites us to meditate on what we will do, or have done, with that precious time. The sun is a *memento mori*, like the skulls that Renaissance thinkers kept on their desks. As we look at the sun we know that after we are gone there will be a billion more sunrises and sunsets over a billion more Earths, just as there were billions before we came into being. But that shouldn't make us feel small or petty or insignificant. After all, we are the ones clever enough to have worked out that the sun is made of burning hydrogen.

conspicuous bringer that is good.

23

Get fit without joining a gym

GYMS ARE A WASTE OF TIME. They exist primarily on the subscriptions of people who never use them.

Everyone can find a piece of rope to use as a skipping rope. Most people have a bike. Most people can jog or walk or do press-ups. These are all perfectly good ways to get fit, and don't rely on you getting all tooled up and driving to a big hall with lots of silly machines in it. A walking machine – could anything be more pointless? Why stare at a wall for half an hour when you could go for an actual walk?

Getting fit can lead to a much better quality of life – even a much better *quantity* of life – and it's definitely worth doing. It's just that it doesn't have to cost anything.

A walking machine — could anything be more pointless?

Some things that you can do to get fit actually produce valuable by-products. Gardening is good exercise and can lead to vegetables. Delivering newspapers is performing a useful service, and you get paid.

'The gym' is a recent fad that relies on the idea that if you throw money at a problem it will go away.

24

Sit still until you see wildlife emerge

'Wildlife' will mean different things according to whether you are a city or a country dweller. But even in towns it is possible to see rabbits, foxes and even deer. Go to a park or university campus and you will almost certainly see rabbits – go to a cemetery and you might see muntjac.

For ordinary suburban dwellers who are willing to sit still for long enough, perhaps the greatest surprise is the bravery of birds. After half an hour of immobility in your deck–chair they will walk right up to you. Blackbirds will come so close that you can see the millimetre-thin ring of orange round their black globes of eyes;

robins and sparrows are brave and plucky enough to peck at scraps of bread or seeds around your feet.

In general, Man enters Nature like a clenched fist. When that fist is slowly unclenched, Nature is remarkably forgiving.

Even in towns it is possible to see rabbits, foxes and even deer.

25

Contact a friend you haven't spoken to for years

'Hey, Alex! It's me, Teresa!'
'Who?'
'Teresa! From school!'
'Oh – my – God! Teresa! How are you?'
'I'm fine!'
'What are you doing with yourself?'
'Well. . . I'm selling this really amazing new product for getting animal hair off clothing!'

Of course, it doesn't have to be like that.

We have all shared things with friends that meant a great deal at the time: secrets, poetry, love, star-gazing, navel-gazing, mountains, holidays, intoxication. But then family responsibilities and work take over. As friendships recede, there is an obscure sense that they will always be there, in cold storage, to be defrosted when time permits. Years pass. Nothing is ever done.

What a waste! You could still be growing together, going on that road trip together, holding that exhibition together, planning that balloon trip together, learning that language together, dreaming together, performing together, laughing together. You could forget all the intervening time, and revive things before it is too late.

Teresa, call me. Better still, I will call you.

As friendships recede, there is an obscure sense that they will always be there, in cold storage.

26

Go cloud-spotting

CLOUD-SPOTTING BECAME an unlikely craze in 2006 after the publication of *The Cloudspotter's Guide* by Gavin Pretor-Pinney (of the Cloud Appreciation Society). But shortly after publication, a new cloud was 'discovered' (even though it had been there all along): this was the Asperatus, which also happens to be one of the most spectacular clouds imaginable. Its strange, billowing down-foldedness has been likened to the patterns made by the breaking of giant waves as seen from underwater. It was as if a new species of buffalo had been discovered living in Piccadilly Circus. If you become a cloud-spotter perhaps you will discover the next new cloud.

endless free spectacle, forming merging disappearing.

Even if you don't, there are numerous reasons to appreciate clouds. They dispense the benedictions of rain and snow. They make wind visible. They provide an endless free spectacle, forming, merging, disappearing, cruising like whales or stretching like dough. They are not merely an impediment to sunshine; they are things of beauty, yet remind us that beauty is transient. They are the denizens of a wilderness above our heads. Contemplating them brings peace to sick souls. They are the most democratic of nature's exhibitions, since all we need to do is look up.

27

Learn to meditate

THERE ARE AS MANY TYPES of meditation as there are sub-types of clouds, and it's not necessary or possible to go into all of them here. The good news is that you don't need a mantra or a guru or a shrine. Meditators really need nothing more than themselves. The converse is that they need nothing less than themselves.

People beginning in meditation are often advised that they should concentrate on the breath – which is good advice. Sit somewhere quiet – the lotus position or any other position is not compulsory – and observe your breath. Direct attention to it, and relax. If your attention wanders from your breathing, bring the attention back. Your attention will definitely drift. (That clock was originally my grandmother's. . .) The important thing is not to get frustrated when it does, and not to think you've failed. Just bring your attention back.

Other people practise an even more minimal form of meditation – sometimes called Raja Yoga meditation – which does not involve concentrating on the breath. It simply consists in sitting somewhere, eyes wide open, and being open to the world and to the thoughts that come. Being in your being, savouring the present moment, feeling the world through your senses, and cutting yourself adrift from plans, responsibilities, work, anxieties. Waiting for an insight – or for nothing.

Then when you return to the world there is a memory of peace inside you and you are less likely to go crazy.

28

Volunteer for something

IF YOU SEE A STRANGER in the road who has had an accident, it's not actually very rational to stop and help them. There are thousands of people suffering in the world, after all. Why should you help this particular one? Why try to stem with your little finger the great tide of misery bursting through the dam of life?

On the other hand, wouldn't you want someone to help you if you were in a similar situation?

To volunteer for something is a decision in favour of the world where someone stops and helps. It's as if to say: 'I want things to be nicer, more loving, more trusting, less suspicious, less mean-spirited, less angry, and this is my small way of helping to achieve this, even if it's only a drop in the bucket.' If enough people think like this, such a world comes to pass.

To volunteer for something is a decision in favour of the world where someone stops and helps.

Volunteering could consist of anything, from looking after the elderly, to cleaning up litter, to conserving wild habitats, to running a mobile library, to cleaning up radioactive waste.

Volunteering is a powerful force for social change – and if you get involved, you are part of that change.

29

Spend a day and night in a forest

BILL BRYSON, in his book *A Walk in the Woods*, gives a pretty scary account of camping out in the forest. He has to deal with everything from the threat of bears to poisoning by mouse dung. But it's not necessary to hike the 2,100 miles of the Appalachian Trail (not that Bryson made it that far) to experience life in the woods. Why not just spend 24 hours out there? It's free. All you need is some form of shelter – a tent being the most obvious. The other paraphernalia of camping – the bulky rucksack, the dried food, the cooking range, the solar-powered TV – can be left for another occasion.

The night is more problematic than the day – the night being when all the sliding, creeping and rustling things come out, things you can hear and not see. But none of them are dangerous (at least where I live). You are Man, destroyer and polluter of worlds. Take a little punishment.

You wake covered in dew, having survived. You eat an individual pecan pie, bundle up your belongings and your rubbish, and walk back to civilization.

you wake

why not just spend 24 hours out there?

covered in dew.

30

Cherish older people

IN WESTERN EUROPE and the USA we currently have a bit of a problem with our attitude to older people. There is a cult of youth that devalues older people and the contribution they can make. Advertising and fashion are the most obvious culprits, but it extends much further. The degree to which things have changed in recent years can be seen most clearly in the realm of politics. Politics was previously the preserve of wise old men. Now it is essential for party leaders to be youthful in order to be electable.

As a result of all this, older people are rendered invisible. They are certainly not considered attractive (except in France, where women of a certain age are worshipped). Neither are they listened to. This is a shame! Older people have lived longer and tend to know a thing or two. For example:

How to enjoy the simple things in life
How to build an Anderson shelter
Why tolerance works better than intolerance
How to skin a rabbit
How to do DIY without killing yourself

Young people on the other hand tend to know less (they are, after all, younger), have more fixed and ill-thought-out opinions, are less considerate, less witty and more likely to vomit over your shoes.

Older people are rendered invisible

31

Reconsider your career

Even if we are enjoying our careers, we

DIANA ATHILL, the writer, publisher and memoirist, now in her nineties, said in an interview in 2009 that she had very few regrets in her life, but one thing she did regret was not changing her career. She had spent a very profitable and pleasurable life in books – meeting many famous people and having lots of fun – but had never taken the opportunity of doing something really different, such as running a restaurant, farming, driving a train or entering politics. These options were now closed to her, and she wished she had had the courage to make at least one career change while she could.

could take a sudden new direction.

Even if we are enjoying our careers and finding them all very fulfilling, it might be worth keeping in the back of our minds the possibility that we could take a sudden new direction. If we don't, will we not feel as Diana Athill did, and wish we'd tried a couple of other things?

To change your career is a big move, may involve a substantial change of life, and possibly a substantial change of income, so it may not be 'free'. On the other hand you might end up richer.

32

Enlarge your comfort zone

IN HER FAMOUS BOOK *Feel the Fear and Do It Anyway*, Susan Jeffers popularized the idea of the 'comfort zone'. The idea goes like this. Most of us spend our lives stuck in routines of thought and behaviour that we have developed because they are comfortable. These may involve our work, our relationships or our social lives. When we are confronted by an opportunity to break out of one of these routines, our first instinct is often not to take it, and to stay in the 'comfort zone'. We value our routines because they have served us so well in the past. They have helped us avoid rejection, pain, disruption and inconvenience. But as a result of our wish to avoid these things, we stop developing as people. We stop having new experiences. We don't grow in our understanding or enjoyment of the world. We stay the same, year after year. And as we go on like this, it becomes increasingly difficult to move out of the zone of familiarity and comfort. Perhaps we started off by choosing to be stuck, but soon we become involuntarily stuck. Paralysis sets in. Life slips by without much fulfilment or enjoyment.

when we are confronted by an opportunity to break out of one of our routines, our first instinct is often not to take it.

Routines are unavoidable for most people, of course. But the idea of the 'comfort zone' acts as a useful corrective in many situations. If you develop the habit of asking yourself: 'Am I turning down this opportunity because it might be uncomfortable if I fail?' you will see where you might be going wrong. Failure is a part of life. Avoidance of failure is avoidance of life.

33

Achieve your
ideal weight

THIS IS DIFFICULT. But the actual method is simplicity itself. It is
this: eat less and exercise more.

To do this you need three things that you probably already have: a
set of bathroom scales, a calorie counter (i.e. a book giving you the
calorific contents of foods; if you don't have one you can find the
information at the library or online) and a blackboard or
notebook.

To lose weight, men should aim to consume about 2,000 calories a
day and women 1,500 calories a day. This will result in a weight
loss, on average, of about 1kg (2lbs) a week. Once you start getting
near your target you will need to consume slightly less, because
your basal metabolic weight will be slowing as you get lighter, but
by this time you will already be quite thin. If you add increased
exercise to this you will lose weight a little faster.

The problem, of course, is managing hunger. The blackboard or
notebook will help. This is to keep a running total of your calorie
count as the day progresses. Without counting it is psychologically

much more difficult to diet. Another tip is to get to know foods that are filling without being calorific: these foods include most fruits and vegetables. A third tip is to reward yourself occasionally by eating things you like (as long as you count them). A fourth tip is to save some small treat for the end of the day.

This all sounds very simplistic, but this is the only information you really need. Don't be suckered by fad diets! There is only one diet: eat less and exercise more.

34

Learn how to talk to strangers in public

PEOPLE LIKE BEING TALKED TO in public, and they like people who make the effort to talk to them (as long as you are not thrusting a leaflet into their hand or a beer can into their face). If you start talking to people as you go about your daily business, it's interesting the things that happen. People smile, they say funny things – you even make friends.

Of course, people can be suspicious. *Why* are you talking to them? What's your hidden motive? Are you trying to chat them up or sell them something?

If you want to learn how to talk to people in public without exciting their suspicion, then an easy way to disarm them is simply to make general observations that don't seem to demand any reply. The longer the observation the better, since longer ones give people time to get over their surprise that you are talking to them. So, in a doctor's waiting room, you could say, with a smile: 'I don't know what it is about radios in waiting rooms – you always get them at the doctor's but never at the accident and emergency. Maybe it's because pop music is more appropriate if you have a cold than if you have a sprained ankle.' Or if you were standing in line at the post office, you could say: 'When I was younger stamps always seemed more interesting, and I used to look forward to the new ones coming out, but for some reason now I don't care what they've got on them any more.'

These are both pretty ordinary observations, but people will be disarmed by your openness, and start talking to you.

35

Visit Project Gutenberg

PROJECT GUTENBERG WAS the first producer of free online electronic books (e-books), and, though there are now many rivals, it still has the best and most comprehensive coverage. The books are all out of copyright, and so most of them will be more than 80 years old, but there are a lot to choose from (over 100,000, in fact); you can take your pick from Charles Dickens, Mark Twain, George Eliot, Jane Austen, William Wordsworth, Lewis Carroll. . . and on and on. They can be read on a PC or Mac or downloaded to read on any handheld device such as a smartphone or Palm organizer.

Project Gutenberg is powered by ideas, ideals, and by idealism.

There is usually a choice of formats so that readers can choose which best suits their requirements in terms of text presentation, download size, and so on. Many of the books come with illustrations. There are now an increasing number of audiobooks, which can be downloaded to a hard-drive or burned onto a CD.

One caveat: these are not 'definitive' texts for people who care a lot about textual variants and the exact placement of semicolons. Project Gutenberg is staffed entirely by volunteers (who transcribe and help distribute the e-books). But the quality is generally exceptionally high.

As Project Gutenberg's mission statement has it: 'Project Gutenberg is powered by ideas, ideals, and by idealism, not by financial or political power. . . We want to provide as many e-books in as many formats as possible for the entire world to read in as many languages as possible. . . Everyone is welcome here at Project Gutenberg.' This is the best of world literature, and it is entirely FREE!

36

Gather a meal from the wild

THERE ARE A NUMBER of guides in print to gathering food from hedgerows and other wild places: they include Richard Mabey's *Food for Free*, Jason Hill's *Wild Foods of Britain* and John Lewis-Stempel's *The Wild Life*, in which he recounts a year living only off things he has shot, picked or dug up. Of course, it's not necessary to live on wild food for any extended period of time, but it is rewarding to try to put a meal together based only on free food.

A good menu for beginners might include any or all of the following: nettle soup (made with stinging nettles, which taste rather like spinach with an aroma reminiscent of shellfish); a salad made of sorrel (a delicious lemony herb with large light green leaves, often found growing on wasteland) mixed with chicory and dandelion leaves; wild mushroom and boiled burdock root (popular in Japan as a vegetable); pigeon, rabbit or squirrel as a meat dish; and, for dessert, wild strawberries, blackberries and other soft fruits.

As far as collecting this food is concerned, hedgerows bordering roads are fair game, as are certain areas of wasteland, common land and woodland. And for those not handy with an air-gun, there is always roadkill. Have look at the *Original Roadkill Cookbook, or Yellow Line Yummies*, by B.R. Peterson.

37

Learn another language

THERE ARE MANY WAYS to learn a language that do not involve paying money to a teacher. Perhaps the best, and the most rewarding way to do it – if you are an English-language speaker – is to make friends with a foreign-language speaker who wants to learn English. You can then learn their language while they learn yours. If this fails, there are other ways: you can borrow language-learning tapes, CDs, DVDs and books from the library. And there are all sorts of language-learning materials online.

The benefits of learning a language are many and varied. You get an insight into another culture. It makes it more fun to go on holiday where the language is spoken. It's a good way of making friends and connections. It brings a powerful sense of achievement. It keeps the brain active. It opens up a new appreciation of a country's literature. It makes you a citizen of the world. It is an antidote to complacency (it's easy for English speakers to be complacent). It brings an appreciation for the struggles of non-English speakers who have to learn English.

And it's entirely free.

It opens up a new appreciation of a country's literature.

38

Invent a language

IF YOU DON'T FANCY learning a language, why not invent one? 'Toki Pona' was invented by Sonja Elen Kisa in 2001. It has only 120 words, so it's pretty easy to learn. It naturally involves quite a lot of doubling up: the word for 'foot' is the same as the word for 'leg', and most flowers have the same name. But even given these restrictions, it's possible to converse in it, and people do. There are message boards on the internet that exclusively use Toki Pona.

You have probably already gone some way to inventing a language. Many people use words that are only really comprehensible to members of their own family. Young children often invent their own names for things. We all naturally enjoy using, abusing and playing with language.

If you want to invent a language, you need to give some thought to matters such as these: whether to include existing words in your language; whether to include existing words from other languages; how many words in total you need; the position of verbs; how many vowels to have; how many consonants; how (and whether) you indicate plurals; how (and whether) you indicate gender; how you form questions; and not a few other things. Resources can be found online, and there are now international bodies devoted to artificially-constructed languages, as well as an annual Language Creation Conference.

In conclusion I will only say *Lirap jan mlulu khorr-khorr,* which in Xunganese means 'Good luck!'

39

Pretend you are a Valet For Humanity™

THE VALET FOR HUMANITY™ Programme is a way of looking at your relationships with other people which consists of asking the simple question, over and over again: what could I do to make this person's life better?

The Valet for Humanity™ Programme doesn't actually exist. But it could! The basic idea is to consider people's feelings and to serve their interests before your own.

Here is an example: a woman goes to a birthday party to collect her child. She walks into the party, finds her child, thanks the parents, and leaves. Standing next to her all the time is the child whose party it was. She has ignored him. The point of the party was to celebrate the child's birthday, but in her self-absorption and desire to get the job done she has missed it. If she had

make this person's life better?

remembered to think of herself as a Valet for Humanity™, and considered other people's feelings, she might not have made this gaffe. Imagine a situation in which she remembered to wish the child a happy birthday. The parents would have been pleased. The child would have been pleased (slightly). She would have felt better about herself. She would have given something. It would have been very, very small, but it would have been important.

The counter-argument to this whole way of looking at the world is that it's somewhat artificial. People are selfish and it's futile to pretend otherwise. Trying to care about others is squeezing a square peg into a round hole, and the effort shows.

But the ultimate choice is between a world in which we try and look after each other, even if it goes against the grain, and a world in which we don't bother.

It seems clear which is better.

40

Go busking

YOU WILL NOT MAKE a great deal of money by busking unless you are spectacularly good: it's probably more about performance than anything else, about getting out there and enjoying yourself.

Busking is yet one more arena

Do you need any musical aptitude? No, not necessarily. You don't need to play an instrument: you could sing. You could even do something entirely different, such as juggling, or reciting poetry. If you decide on the latter, choose your poetry wisely. Crowd-pleasers such as Kipling's 'If' or Tennyson's 'The Charge of the Light Brigade' will produce the best results.

To be a successful busker the professionals suggest a number of things. Pitch somewhere where you can be seen and heard a long way off, so that people have time to make a decision as to whether to give you something (and how much). Pick your act with care to appeal to mass taste. 'Salt' your case or hat with a little money to show people what's expected of them. Busking in front of people sitting outside, for example at a restaurant, is an option for the seasoned busker, and may have good results if you have a personable hat-man or hat-woman to collect for you.

Busking is yet one more arena where you may find out a little more about what it means to be you. If you feel shy about being you, you can do it with a group of friends.

where you may find out a little more about what it means to be you.

41

Start a book in which to record things that have really, really made you laugh

ARTHUR KOESTLER related laughter to the moment of discovery and to the appreciation of beauty; Freud linked it to the unconscious; Henri Bergson to the unexpected yoking of different worldviews. Whatever the truth, when we laugh we surrender ourselves to a very mysterious force. We act as if possessed or in the grip of some drug: we make involuntary noises, we throw back our heads, screw up our faces, or roll on the ground. This is among the most primal of experiences, simultaneously deeply physical and profoundly linked to our humanity. Laughter takes us over, holds us, then lets us go. Where does it go to? Perhaps we should mark its passing.

Laughter takes us over,

A laughter diary is a book recording things that have really, really made you laugh. Not social laughs, but moments of unexpected hilarity, when suddenly you are caught up in the absurdity and brilliance of life. In a way, that's what any diary should be about: recording those moments when you feel truly alive. Certainly they make the best reading afterwards.

holds us, then lets us go.

42

Go somewhere outdoors that is very silent

IN THE NOISIEST TOWNS, the ambient sound generated by day-to-day activities is around the same as an alarm clock ringing constantly in the face – around 80 decibels. At 120 decibels, human ears experience pain. In 2009, Deepak Prasher, Professor of Audiology at University College London, wrote: 'Noise pollution in our towns and cities is a growing problem and can have a serious long-term impact on our health and well-being. Noise not only annoys but also can raise our stress levels and associated hormone levels.' It has also been found by researchers in Germany that high levels of ambient noise can increase the risk of heart attack and stroke and lead to hearing damage.

With this in mind it might be an idea to seek out somewhere quiet, away from the hum of computers, traffic, noisy pubs, restaurants, etc., to remember what silence actually sounds like.

Away from urban centres there are still places in the world where you can hear your own breath rise and fall. Places such as moorlands on windless days register zero on an audiometer, with only the occasional rustle of an insect or chirp of a bird to agitate the needle. Stress lessens. Anger abates. Suddenly it becomes easier to think.

43

Make Christmas presents for your whole family one year

Children can probably get away with this more easily than adults. The fact that they have spent any time and effort on making a Christmas present rather than just buying it in a shop (probably with their parents' money) is very touching.

For adults, however, a little more sophistication and originality is called for. Something that will have the recipients shrieking with delight and surprise as they open their presents and yet will be free to make, or as close to free as humanly possible. How to achieve it? A few ideas to start you off:

*   A nude calendar of yourself to a loved one. Set up the shots, employ tasteful props such as plants, obelisks, etc. Don't forget they might hang it up where visitors can see it! Calendar blanks are available from newsagents.

*   Casts in soap. These can be in any shape whatsoever, the more unexpected the better. Try casting your own hand (so that when they wash themselves they will be washing *with your hand*). Soap-casting materials are cheap and can be bought at craft shops.

Something that will have the recipients shrieking with delight and surprise.

- A painting or drawing of their house. You can do this from a photo, either from outside or inside their house. For added interest you can put the gift recipient in the picture, or anything else – a bear, a dinosaur, a giant foot.

- Home-made alcohol, such as beer, wine or cider. This requires some preparation but is very cheap, and can be given to every adult of your acquaintance. Spend time creating an amusing label.

44

Give something up

THERE'S AN EPISODE of the US sitcom *Seinfeld* in which Kramer (Jerry Seinfeld's neighbour) gives up cooking – he decides to eat only raw food. When asked why, he says: 'You know, I've discovered I enjoy depriving myself of things!'

I need not warn anyone of the dangers of smoking and drinking. I will confine myself to observing that giving things up – living more simply, reducing one's needs – is satisfying in and of itself. Not from a moral point of view (because waste is bad, because TV is harming the planet, etc.) but just because it is not always a good idea to have all one's desires satisfied. Just as the greatest disaster for any young person can be getting what they want too early, so a life full of self-gratification may be one lived ultimately without appetite, without savour.

Our lives tend to be very smooth, like well-surfaced roads. When a pothole comes up we are sometimes not ready for it. That is, unless we have deliberately travelled along roads with potholes.

45

Cheer up lonely men in public places

NEXT TIME you are in a big city, try looking for single guys with haunted expressions – otherwise known as Haunted Male Pedestrians (or HMPs). You will see quite a few of them. They're not noticeably down and out: merely lost, shifty and at a loose end. Now try looking for single women with the same haunted expressions. There aren't so many, are there? The women all seem to be striding along purposefully in the pursuit of work, or strolling along amiably in the pursuit of shopping or children. They appear to know what they're doing.

But these HMPs don't. They don't have friends, at least none in this part of town. They don't have cars. They don't have work. They are drifting around looking for a sandwich, haunted by their failures, their abandoned children, their disappointments. They need a boost. And you can give it to them.

When you see one, say to him: 'You're looking good!' or 'That's a nice shirt!' or 'I see good luck coming your way!'

46

Swap your CDs

THERE ARE NUMEROUS places online where you can swap things. Usually you have to pay a small charge per item swapped, plus postage. So this is not an entirely free activity.

Here's a twist on the idea that *is* free – and has some other benefits. Make a list of all the CDs you don't really want (or books, or DVDs) and put them all on one sheet of paper. Put your name, address and contact details on the piece of paper, explain that you want to swap your stuff, copy the sheet and post it through all the doors in your road. Anyone who wants any of your CDs (or books, etc.) can reply by posting you a list of all the things that they no longer want to keep. You can then choose from among them, contact the person and make the trade.

As more and more people join in, you will have several lists of stuff to choose from. You could then start a website to keep the lists updated. The difference between such a website and an ordinary one would be that it would be a sort of 'intranet' for your street – one that none of the people in your street would have heard about unless they'd been invited on paper.

As a result you get new CDs, it doesn't cost anything, and you finally meet your neighbours!

47

Adopt or invent a personal motto

SOME EXAMPLES of traditional 'heraldic' mottos:

> Bring forth what is in you.
> Truth above all.
> Pride in humility, wealth in generosity.
> As long as I breathe, I hope.

Some more modern personal mottos:

> Remember who you wanted to be.
> Do one thing every day that scares you.
> Ask permission afterwards.
> A closed mouth gathers no foot.

To create a personal motto, you could adopt a quotation or a saying that you've heard, but the best approach is probably to invent one of your own. Spend some time thinking about the wisdom you've managed to garner over the years, the kind of person you are, and what your hopes and aspirations are. If nothing occurs, think about the moment you were proudest of yourself, and try to define why. For example, if you once stopped a bully, your motto could be: 'Defend the weak.'

If your motto is powerful, resonant, and personal, it will apply to the whole of your life, and you can chant it to yourself when the going gets rough.

48

Support your
local eccentric

PEOPLE WHO BUILD FOLLIES, people who talk to their fellow passengers on the bus, deadbeat artists, owners of pet lobsters, people who smoke meerschaum pipes, people who don't own a television, skip-rats, people of both sexes who cultivate unusual facial hair, surrealists, people who refuse to recognize the terms AD and BC, people who revel in the fact that other people laugh at them: these are good people to gravitate towards if you want to have your view of the world refreshed.

In a recent study, *Eccentrics: A Study of Sanity and Strangeness*, Dr David Weeks made some surprising findings. Eccentrics, he discovered, were generally healthier than the rest of the populace. They were more likely to be gifted and creative. They were more curious and idealistic than those around them. Far from suffering a greater degree of mental illness, they were generally psychologically more healthy than the rest of us, as a result (Dr Weeks hypothesized) of the lower stress brought about by their lack of any urgent desire to conform.

In many communities there is a low tolerance for eccentrics: they are perceived as posing a threat to respectability, contributing nothing useful to society or driving down property values. If you have the chance, defend them. We need them.

Eccentrics are generally healthier than the rest of the populace.

49

Become a freegan

IN MY FIRST HOUR of freeganism, or 'dumpster-diving' outside supermarkets, I found:

- two large punnets of strawberries, in perfect condition, eat-by date tomorrow

- one punnet of apricots, in perfect condition, eat-by date unspecified (but very tasty)

- several green apples, loose, in excellent condition

- one child's football-themed birthday cake, packaged and sealed, very large, iced, sell-by date today

- a sealed packet of basil, perfectly edible, eat-by date tomorrow

- several loose bananas, slight bruising

- a packet of luxury chocolate brownies, sealed, sell-by date next week, each individually cellophane-wrapped, perfect condition

- numerous packets of sealed bread rolls, sell-by date today, perfect condition

... and I could go on indefinitely. Suffice it to say I found enough in an hour to feed myself for a week. All of the food, except for the loose fruit, was individually wrapped and sealed. Someone at the supermarket had even placed the food in individual clear plastic bags, which made it easier to see what was inside each one.

A couple of tips: supermarkets offer good pickings, but sandwich bars and other places may also be worth a look. Some premises lock their bins or keep them in locked enclosures, though not all. The best time for scavenging is at the end of the day.

The amount of waste going on is quite shocking.

50

Swim in the sea

A LONG SWIM IN THE SEA can leave you feeling very refreshed and relaxed. The freedom from gravity among the waves and tides is an elemental experience not available in a swimming-pool. Another advantage is that in the sea you usually have enough room to keep swimming without constantly looking ahead to see you are not going to crash into someone or something. Swimming is the only sport where it helps if you're fat (long-distance swimmers find that a bit of blubber floats them higher out of the water and makes it easier to propel themselves forward); and if you want to make sea-swimming a serious part of your holiday you can even book trips that consist of just swimming from one island to another, with boat support. Travel and accommodation notwithstanding, sea-swimming is entirely free (and easy to do if you live on an island like Britain).

There are a few caveats: make sure you understand the flag systems on beaches – a red flag will usually mark where it is unsafe to swim. Try and swim where there is a lifeguard. Check the weather reports before you go out and beware of the tides. Be careful of sunburn in hot weather and hypothermia in cold. Don't trail a bag of fish intestines after you.

the waves and tides is an elemental experience.

Get to know your neighbours

Getting to know your neighbours could improve your life. You might make new friends. You might improve the general safety of your area. It could lead to the pooling of resources (such as car journeys or garden produce).

But it's hard to make the first move.

Getting to

Here are some suggestions:

- Have a coffee morning. Make up flyers, get in a supply of tea, coffee and biscuits, and await results. Alternatively organize a wine and cheese evening – or a beer and pretzels evening.
- Have a barbecue. If you don't want to host it, find a piece of common land and organize a joint barbecue.
- Tidy up your local area together.
- Organize a local history walk.
- If you have an area of common land, organize a traditional fête with sports and games.
- If you know of anyone in your street who has a special talent – such as watercolour painting or belly-dancing – organize free evenings where the expert can share some of their knowledge.
- Match people with unused back gardens to people who need more land (see page 140).
- Swap your CDs, books or other stuff (see page 88).

Know your neighbours could improve your life

52

Act without expecting anything back

Is THERE such a thing as an unselfish act?

Take the example of a man who donates blood, and tells no one what he has done. He doesn't get paid and the recipient can never thank him. Nevertheless he feels good; he feels that he has acted in accordance with his moral principles. This is his pay-off, then: he feels good. So has he really acted unselfishly?

This is a conundrum as old as philosophy. Altruism, some say, is impossible. There must be a benefit to any action, and it is hard to imagine anyone committing an altruistic act that made them feel worse about themselves. Even those who go so far as to die for others are perhaps demonstrating that they couldn't live with themselves if they didn't.

But look at it for a moment in terms of *results*, not in terms of moral philosophy. People who do good without expecting anything for themselves – apart from a good feeling – create a more generous society where it is generally nicer to live. They may also unshackle themselves substantially from disappointment and resentment. Once you stop expecting a return, there is none of the sense of injustice which comes with adding things up on a tit-for-tat basis. You are better able to act naturally and easily in your relationships with others.

To act without expecting anything back can be therefore be personally liberating as well as creating a more friendly world to live in.

people who do good create a better society

Deliver meals on wheels

THE 'WHEELS' OF MEALS ON WHEELS were originally pram wheels: meals were delivered in baby carriages under bales of straw to keep them hot.

Delivering meals to people in need is about much more than food.

Meals on Wheels schemes, under different names – in the 1950s in the USA they were known as 'Platter Angels' – are usually run by volunteers, who work as drivers, deliverers, or in the office as administrators or in food preparation and packing. Most of the recipients these days tend to be elderly, but others have learning difficulties or problems shopping for or preparing food. Anyone over 18 can volunteer, and hours are usually flexible – a couple of hours a week is quite usual. Transport may be provided. To volunteer you can contact your local voluntary services centre. In Britain Meals on Wheels are often run by the local WRVS (Women's Royal Voluntary Service).

Delivering meals to people in need is about much more than food. The volunteer provides a social contact and makes the recipient feel valued. Volunteers notice if anything unusual is going on, and will contact friends or relatives if the recipient doesn't answer the door. People who get meals delivered to them are better able to live independent lives in their own homes. For the volunteer, too, it can be a life-changing experience. In fact, it may be the deliverer who benefits most.

54

Look for glue

Glue, actually is everywhere around us, and we are all

IN AN INTERVIEW for the BBC in 2009, Marina Lewycka (the author of *A Short History of Tractors in Ukrainian*), talked about the genesis of her novel *We Are All Made of Glue*. It began with a visit from a fan, Ewen Kellar. 'Ewen came along and sat in my office,' she said, 'and asked me to sign some books for him, and told me that he was an adhesives chemist. And I thought – goodness, what could be more frightfully boring than that? And then I thought, that's a bad attitude, because all around us life is made up of things that seem to be boring but are actually very important. Glue, actually, is everywhere around us, and we are all made of glue, quite literally – skin and bones, boil them down, and glue is what you get.' Soon, as the author learned more, the varieties of glue became a major strand of her novel-in-progress. The heroine became a writer for a magazine called *Adhesives in the Modern World*, and in the book's closing pages were the words: 'I understand now that everything – whales and dolphins, Palestinians and Jews, stray cats, rainforests, mansions and mining villages – they're all interconnected, held together by some mysterious force – call it glue, if you like.'

made of glue, quite literally.

What Marina Lewycka found in glue is available everywhere.
Look at any item of modern manufacturing: a plastic bag, a toilet
roll, reading glasses, anything. Or any natural object: a leaf, a
peach-stone, a puddle. If you look hard enough, it quickly
becomes apparent that there is no such thing as an ordinary object.
Things are full of secrets.

Send a message in a bottle

At one time it was fashionable to send "balloon letters" until it was pointed out that deflated balloons can disfigure the landscape, and if they fall into the sea can be a hazard to marine life. So, instead of sending a message on a balloon, why not try the traditional method of sending a message in a bottle? Glass bottles are best – glass is an inert material and cannot pollute (glass is essentially sand).

Stories of people finding messages in bottles and then meeting the person who has sent it, falling in love, getting married and having children who then go on to send their own messages in bottles are too numerous to list. Perhaps it would be good simply to restrict this to practicalities:

- Use a glass bottle with a cork (metal caps rust).

- Release into an outgoing tide.

- Include some stamps or an email address.

- Don't make your message too complicated or specific; anyone might find it – a child, an old man, or someone who doesn't speak English.

- Date your message.

- Include in the bottle something other than a note, if you wish – for example, a computer memory stick with some pictures on it. Hopefully it won't wash up on a desert island where the only inhabitant does not have a computer.

- If you don't live near an ocean, release your bottle into a river or canal, or even leave it on land – on a park bench, in a supermarket – for someone to find.

56

Have an eco-friendly bonfire

THERE IS SOMETHING PRIMAEVAL about a bonfire. We all feel it when we gather around a fire on a cold winter's night. Bonfires play a central role in Wiccan celebrations, and in the Burning Man festival in the Black Rock Desert of Nevada the centrepiece is a huge combustible 'wicker man'. This is an activity that stirs something deep within us.

If you want to have one of your own it's worth making it environmentally-friendly. The Wiccans would approve. For example, don't burn things such as plastic, treated wood, tyres, paint or chemicals. They give off poisonous fumes and are unpleasant. Also be aware of what might be in household rubbish – aerosol cans can go off with a bang. Instead use dry garden waste, branches, dead wood, and untreated wood. And don't forget to make the bonfire friendly to animals (such as hedgehogs who might take refuge in the stack) or pets (who might prefer to be inside the house).

Now get some friends round. Call them from far and wide. Call someone who can sing (see page 16), someone who can recite poetry (see page 24) or do tricks (see page 160). Praise the bonfire-stack in verse, prose and song. Then set a match to it. The heat, the screams, the excitement on children's faces!

...the excitement on children's faces!

Attempt a world record

As I write, the world record for juggling running chainsaws is set at an absurdly low number of catches – 86. This is surely ripe for a record attempt. The world record for balancing spoons on the face – 16 spoons – is currently held by a 9-year-old boy, and it stands to reason that if an adult tried it, having a larger face area, the record would be broken. The world record for highest jump by a pig is only 70cm, on Mokumoku Tedsukuri Farm, Mie, Japan. Couldn't anyone train a pig to do better than that?

Opportunities abound in almost every area. Guinness World Records have over 30,000 different record categories on their database. Many of them require very little or no equipment. There are world records for eating cockroaches, typing books backwards, running barefoot on ice, driving through the smallest gap, writing on the back of a postage stamp, pogo-stick jumping up the CN Tower in Toronto, Wellington-boot racing and simultaneous Scrabble playing. To have your record verified all you need to do is to send off for a record verification pack from the people at Guinness World Records.

Wouldn't it be fun to be the best in the world at something?

wouldn't it be fun to be the best in the world at something?

58

Walk in the rain

BEING IN THE RAIN can be extraordinarily pleasurable, even sensual. Once you have accepted that you are going to get splashed, dripped, showered and trickled upon, a new world of possibilities opens up. During a rainstorm you may find that the streets are deserted: humanity is in retreat from nothing more hostile than water. You – who have realized that rain is completely harmless – will have the place to yourself. Go with a friend or someone special, just the two of you. Rain seems to foster confidences. There is a new smell in the air, especially if you catch the storm just as the heavens break after a dusty day. Greenery takes on a new lushness.

walking in the rain is an elemental experience in every sense.

Walking in the rain is an elemental experience in every sense.
Children know this, and run with wild shrieks into rain, dancing
and splashing in puddles.

It's possible to survive a rainstorm without getting wet, if you so
desire, by employing umbrellas, overshoes, hats, mackintoshes,
plastic trousers, Wellington boots. But is this not to insulate oneself
against the primal, the elemental?

As Philip Larkin said: 'If I were called in/ To construct a religion/
I should make use of water.'

59

Give away free trees

THIS IS COMPLETELY FREE – and yet could result in a big difference to your neighbourhood.

The idea is to raise trees from saplings and give them away to anyone who wants one. Effectively you are raising trees to be planted in other people's gardens. If you give away enough, your whole area will slowly become greener.

Saplings are best raised not from seeds or acorns but from cuttings. These should be taken after leaf fall when the sap is low. Snip a section off last year's new growth, using a diagonal cut. A dip in a little hormone rooting powder helps, though this is not essential. Pot it up in a general purpose compost. Leave the cuttings out during the winter under some minimal protection, such as a corrugated plastic cloche. Make sure they don't dry out. For hardwood cuttings (such as willow, oak, poplar, aspen, etc.) no heating is required. Roots will appear the following spring. These saplings can then be grown on until they are ready to give away.

Put a notice in your window: 'FREE SAPLINGS!'

60

Do a sponsored parachute/bungee jump

TO JUMP OUT of a plane or off a high bridge for the first time, trusting only to a parachute that you have never seen open, or a piece of elastic that might well break, is to achieve a moment of clarity not generally available in day-to-day life. At the point when you make the decision to throw yourself into nothingness, suddenly there is only you. Your job, your family, your loves and hates, fall away; the peripheral parts are lost and there is only you, the you-ness of you, at the point of decision, at the brink of a void of whistling air. You leap; your blood screams; you scream; the spectators scream; voluntarily you are a fragment, a seed, a plummeting human spore.

And if you sort out your sponsorship beforehand, it's entirely free.

61

Perform

Think noisily and colourfully or you're not alive.

VACHEL LINDSAY was one of the great poets of American
egalitarianism. He got his start through a suggestion from his art
teacher, Robert Henri. In March 1905 Lindsay was urgently in
need of money, and asked Henri if he would ever cut it as an artist.
Henri tactfully replied that he would do better trying to sell his
poetry. Lindsay, either in desperation or inspiration, rushed off
some copies of his poems and took them onto the streets of
Manhattan. Pricing the poems at two cents each, he earned 15
cents on the first day (one doctor paid 5 cents for two poems) –
and was elated. After binding his oeuvre into the collection
Rhymes to be Traded for Bread, he began a series of tramps all
over America bartering recitals for food and shelter. He became
famous, read for Woodrow Wilson, was praised by Yeats, and
published several further collections.

Vachel Lindsay had decided he could not confine the art surging
within him. He needed to express himself by any means necessary.
Often he met with no success, and gave his poems away free. Still
he persisted. What his experience showed is that there is always
someone who is willing to listen if you stick your neck out.

To perform – music, dance, poetry – is one of the joys of life. As Mel Brooks put it: 'You must at least think noisily and colourfully, or you're not alive.'

62

Cycle 100 miles in a day

This is pretty tough but not impossible. And there's a real sense of achievement in pulling off such a feat of endurance.

To minimize the suffering, bear in mind the following points:

- You need to train. Cycle 10 miles or more per day for a week or two beforehand. In the days leading up to the attempt, cycle 25 miles or more per day. On the day before the attempt, rest.

- Don't train on a stationary bike. Train on the bike you are going to use for the attempt.

- Use a bike that is suitable for road-racing, not a mountain bike (the tyres create drag).

- Familiarize yourself with the basic workings of your bike. Take basic tools and spares to repair your bike on the road.

- Plan your route and avoid hills if possible. Don't get lost! Quiet roads are the best. Avoid rush hour if you can.

- Make the attempt in summer when you have more daylight hours to complete the 100 miles. A reasonable average is 10 miles an hour (including breaks), which will take you ten hours.

- Fit your bike with a milometer so you will know for certain that you have achieved the 100 miles.

- Protect yourself against sunburn.

- Take plenty of food and water. Five litres of water is about right. Drink regularly – every half an hour at the very least. You will also need to consume a great deal of high-energy food such as chocolate bars, bananas, etc.

63

Serenade someone

THIS RELIES ON a certain subtlety. You are doing this to please another person, the love of your life. So if they are easily embarrassed, don't start belting out 'You are the Sunshine of My Life' in a crowded restaurant. A soft rendition in private, or perhaps on a park bench, would be better. Or you could call them up and do it over the phone – even leaving it on their answerphone. The key is sincerity. Practice your song, polish it, make sure you know all the words and that you can carry the tune, and then put everything you've got into it. Sing it like you mean it.

Make sure your song isn't too long – if the serenade isn't going too well, you might welcome the chance of an easy exit. Choose the song wisely to fit your loved one's known tastes. You could also bring an instrument of some kind. If you don't play anything, perhaps a tambourine.

If you are planning a balcony serenade, deceive the person into standing on the balcony, make a quick excuse to get away, then run outside and surprise him or her. If only the full balcony serenade will do, and the serenade is scheduled to take place at your lover's home, choose a lover who does not live in a basement.

64

Reflect on something you're grateful for

MOST READERS of this book will be living a life of astonishing material richness. Our ancestors didn't have electrical power to run machines to do work for them and supply bright light anytime they wanted it, nor the ability to speak to friends anywhere in the globe: in fact they didn't always have sufficient

To appreciate something while we have it may lead to a better overall quality of life

food, nor running, potable water (let alone that most extravagant of all human luxuries, hot running water). These are what we now call 'basic' needs: food, water, shelter, power. More important even than these, though, are surely the human things: family, loving relationships, good health, peace, friends, community. But, as with our material wealth, we tend to take them all for granted. It's only when some disaster robs us of one of them that we realize what we've lost.

To appreciate something while we have it may lead to a better overall quality of life. We may stop fixating on what we want, which can make us envious. If we're in the habit of reflecting on the things we have and are grateful for, it may even salve a little of the pain when they are taken away. We may be better able to say to ourselves: 'Yes, it was good then, but even without [insert thing that has been taken away] there is still so much to be grateful for.'

65

Cook and eat a nine-course meal

YOU SIMPLY NEED eight friends. Ask each of them to supply a course. Each friend is then assigned to one of the nine courses. You yourself provide the hospitality and one of the courses. Bring the whole thing together and you have a nine-course meal. The fact that you have to supply one of the courses means that this is not *entirely* free, but you would have been eating anyway. And you'll be buying in bulk!

In traditional French cooking, the nine courses might comprise: 1) an introductory dish, also called an '*amuse-bouche*'; 2) fish; 3) seafood (such as scallops or mussels); 4) *foie gras*; 5) soup; 6) lobster; 7) meat; 8) cheese; 9) dessert. Another variant with Italian components might run: 1) appetizer; 2) soup; 3) salad; 4) *antipasto* (e.g. seared peppers on toasted bread); 5) meat; 6) pasta; 7) dessert: 8) cheese; 9) brandy and cigars. A Japanese theme might replace any of the above with sushi, sashimi, tofu, noodles, etc. It's really up to you.

Discuss their choices with your guests beforehand and print a little menu. Don't tell the others what the courses are going to be, so that the whole meal is a surprise.

66

Write a love letter

IN FUTURE YEARS there will be no love emails in biscuit tins in the wardrobe. Therefore, to ensure that your letter will endure forever, you must write it on paper, preferably in your own hand.

A love letter could really be anything, from the simple written statement 'I love you' (hard to improve upon; see *Nineteen Eighty-Four* by George Orwell) to an entire book, written for, published and dedicated to your love. It could be written to your partner of 50 years, or to someone you have never met. It might recall where you first met; how your feelings for that person are unique and never to be repeated; how they will endure. But it should tell of your feelings in language that is all your own. It should avoid the flowery, the clichéd and the fancy. It might be funny or whimsical, but should be real, should be identifiably from you and only you. This means that using someone else's words or poetry is not really a good idea.

Another approach is to memorize the letter, and instead of sending it, recite it. This works as a declaration of love, and can also work as an affirmation of love. You should probably not recite it parrot-fashion word-for-word, but memorize the main points, then find an appropriate moment and tell your loved one what is in your heart.

It should tell of your feelings in language that is all your own.

67

Create a lair

A LAIR IS THE HOLE of an animal. The lair of a human being is a place where they may be animalistic. In it they may hide from the world, hunker down, plot, and do unspeakable things.

Children create lairs quite naturally – they crawl into spaces adults cannot go, construct dens made from stepladders and cloth, build bracken-shrouded retreats in the forest, tree-houses, hide-outs in the attic. Just because people grow up doesn't mean that the desire to do these things goes away. That's why the secret underground base of the villain in the James Bond films has such a primal appeal – and the fact that it's underground is significant. Our desire to withdraw into a solitary retreat, from which we may dominate the world, is buried in the id, the submerged, unregenerate part of adult consciousness. American men have 'dens': so should we all.

The decoration of your lair will be up to you: thick cloths, soft cushions, rich fabrics are recommended, as are enclosed spaces and strict privacy. A bank of TV screens may be helpful.

68

Notice beauty

WHICH IS almost everywhere.

It seems that beauty and love are waiting for you to notice them. When you find them you can't understand why they were so shy, and you so stupid. Then you notice in the faces of strangers that they too know the secret. And in those faces there is no furious desire, only the innocent satiety of being in a world of such abundant loveliness.

Beauty, amazingly, is entirely free. What a strange state of affairs! We expend a fortune on trash and the real wealth is everywhere, unbuyable.

69

Let go of emotional pain

Life brings painful emotional experiences: broken relationships, betrayal, anger, disappointment, loss and death. It is impossible to be alive and not experience them. However, there are marked differences in how people cope with this pain. Some experience it and recover; others experience it and then hold onto it, continuing to experience the pain for years, or decades, or for their whole life. They have what is commonly termed 'baggage'.

It is not a good idea to embrace pain as a part of one's life.

Hanging on to emotional pain may lead to very real and serious ill-effects. For example, people may be left so distrustful that they are unable to form new relationships. They may seek relief in alcohol or drugs, or try to recreate the experience that has left them in such pain, in order to exorcise it. Pain can come out in depression or suicide. Holding on to pain is by no means risk-free.

What to do? Obviously such a complex problem is outside the scope of this book. One piece of advice the present author can offer is that it is not a good idea to embrace pain as a part of one's life. For the sake of one's own well-being, one should not set up a shrine to pain; its worship will ultimately be damaging. The people who recover from emotional pain tend to be the ones who, after taking time to explore it, talk about it, and perhaps express their feelings creatively, then affirm themselves and their value, separate themselves from the pain, and finally say goodbye to it. They recognize that holding on to pain has the power to limit them, and so they reject it. Without this insight, healing is impossible.

70

Write down your parents' or grandparents' stories

Every life contains something remarkable. Sometimes it is obviously remarkable, and sometimes it requires some investigation to tease out. Your parents have produced you and therefore they are remarkable. Your grandparents by the same logic are doubly remarkable.

At first they will say: 'There's nothing remarkable about my life'. This is untrue. They simply don't want to talk about it. What was it like when they first fell in love, 80 years ago? What was it that led them to move to Nova Scotia? Why were they on television? When was that? During the disaster? What disaster? And so on.

Your parents and grandparents

Your parents and grandparents have lived through amazing times. What was it like to be alive in the Cold War? The Vietnam War? The Second World War? What was the effect of these conflicts on morals? What extraordinary things did their friends do? Who died, and in what circumstances? The stories will come pouring out. You will have enough material for 50 books. You'll get a little closer to your parents or your grandparents and you'll have stories to tell anyone who wants to listen.

have lived through amazing times.

71

Look at your day-to-day concerns from the point of view of five years from now

HAVE YOU EVER had the experience of finding an old 'to–do' list?
One that you wrote many months or years ago? If so, it's likely
that you have forgotten about most of the things on it. 'Call Mum.'
'Get eye test.' 'See teacher.' These were real and pressing concerns

at the time: you may have dreaded that call to Mum, were worried you couldn't afford those new glasses, or were eating yourself up about a bully at your child's school. Now all these anxieties have drifted off like wind-blown fluff. They have been replaced by new anxieties: now, today, your computer has crashed, you've lost files, your work has been halted, your bank account is low, your teeth need attention, your car is making a strange noise. And yet these problems, in their turn, will pass. In five years you won't even remember why you were worried.

If you try to develop the habit of seeing your day-to-day concerns from the point of view of five years in the future, you will gain one valuable and obvious thing – perspective. You will still need to deal with your present problems, of course – your bank account will not miraculously fill up by itself – but you will see the problems for what they are, i.e. not life-or-death crises but temporary hurdles which in their turn will be replaced by new hurdles. A new sense of calm will come. You will see that problems are part of life, that they will keep coming, and coming, and coming, inevitably, for as long as you are vitally involved in the world, and that you will handle them, and handle them, and handle them, just as you always have before.

If you try to develop the habit of seeing your day to day concerns from the point of view of five years in the future, you will gain one valuable and obvious thing – perspective.

72

Fan the flames of desire

YOU WANT TO BE a model.

Go ahead, then, be one!

You want to start a charity to protect tuna from the mayonnaise industry.

Fine, God speed, I'm right behind you!

The key to success in anything, the *sine qua non*, is this: desire.

If you really want something more than anything else, so that thoughts of it occupy you ceaselessly and you cannot imagine happiness without it, then eventually, if you work hard for it, in a free democracy in peacetime, it is very likely that you will get it.

If on the other hand you would just 'sort of' like it, if it would be 'nice', and if you're waiting till the kids grow up till you get around to it, it is very likely that you will not get it.

Everything flows from desire. The greatest things flow from the greatest desires. If you want a castle in Spain, the grandeur of your desire must match the grandeur of the castle. Money, blueprints, estate agents, architects: all these are secondary.

73

Contemplate imperfection and impermanence as forms of beauty

YOSHIDA KENKO was a Japanese monk of the fourteenth century who wrote a book called the *Tsurezuregusa*, sometimes translated into English as 'Essays in Idleness'. It became enormously influential on the development of Japanese culture and is still studied in Japanese schools. Its way of looking at the world is one perhaps not readily comprehensible to people living in the West, particularly its vision of imperfection and impermanence as forms of beauty.

Kenkou writes, for example, about standing in the overgrown garden of a ruined house. He muses on the inevitable decay of earthly things. Suddenly he sees an arm emerge from behind a broken screen in the house, and realizes that there is someone still living there; he is overwhelmed by the beauty of the moment. Or he contemplates a broken pot and wonders whether the clean lines of a perfectly-executed pot are not too cool, unsuggestive and alien to human experience.

Our lives are full of imperfection, and they don't last very long; and yet we only call those works of art or nature beautiful which are 'perfected' as far as possible. We tend to admire magnificent sunsets rather than a pond choked by weeds. And yet if we are to reclaim our own flawed lives as beautiful, mustn't we also re-evaluate the choked pond? Mustn't we also see beauty in the irregular and incomplete, the humble and simple, the incipient and fading, the impermanent and imperfect?

74

Join a gardening scheme where only your labour is required

A NEW MOVEMENT has sprung up recently which is a sort of internet-dating service for horticulturalists. The idea is to match landowners – anyone from farmers to people with a big back garden – to growers who need land. For example, a school allotment might need volunteers to help keep it in shape over the summer; or an older person might wish to turn part of their garden over to enthusiastic growers who will undertake to mow the lawn in exchange for the fruits of the earth. The landowners

Growers are much more involved as directors and managers of the final result.

get their land developed at no cost, and the growers get fed. And it's not limited to vegetables: chickens, pigs, ducks and goats can be raised, and entire farms are beginning to be run this way, essentially with free labour supplied by landless enthusiasts with time on their hands and a desire to get back to nature. The difference between this new movement and movements of the past which offered, say, working weekends on organic farms, is that growers are much more involved as directors and managers of the final result – choosing which vegetables to plant, or which livestock to keep. In many cases no tools, seeds or any other equipment are required of the growers. The landowner supplies everything, and all the grower supplies is his or her labour. Which makes it all entirely free.

Laugh in the face of death

MODERN WARFARE, it is often said, has eroded the distinction between combatant and civilian: now we are all combatants. More civilians are dying in Iraq or Afghanistan than soldiers, and more civilians died in the Second World War or the Vietnam War than any of the people with guns. In the Cold War everyone, young and old, waited listlessly for a holocaust in which humanity itself would be extirpated: the whole world was a war zone, and Death could quite rationally be thought of not as an event that would occur at the terminus of an allotted three score years and ten, but at any time, in any place. The only sane response was to laugh – as Stanley Kubrick did in *Doctor Strangelove*.

But the state of affairs that obtains during such a conflict is not so dissimilar from the state of affairs of human existence in general. We are thrown into the world without being consulted, and, except in the case of suicides, will be taken from it without being consulted. As before, the only way through life is to laugh at the absurdity of it all – an existence that is simultaneously beautiful, fascinating, surprising, uncertain, painful and boring.

If you're not convinced, consider this joke: Two detectives were investigating the murder of Juan Gonzalez. 'How was he killed?' asked the first detective. 'With a golf gun,' the second replied. 'A golf gun? What's that?' asked the first detective. 'I don't know,' said the second. 'But it sure made a hole in Juan.'

76

Train your memory

Memory experts will tell you

THIS IS FREE to do, and can change your life. A good memory will enhance your social skills, and is vital in language learning, academic work, complex job operations, and so on.

Memory experts will tell you that the key to remembering anything is association. If you make a mental link between the thing you want to remember and another object or idea, a magical neural chemistry springs into action. Try it with any important number, such as the one on the front of your credit card. Break the number down into two-digit segments. Assign each of the segments to a year, and think of something that happened in that year. So, if the first four numbers are '4539', you might think of the

that the key to remembering anything is association.

date of the end of the Second World War, '45' (i.e. 1945) and the date of its beginning, '39' (i.e. 1939). Now go through the entire number making connections with years and relating them to one another in a similar way.

Names of people can be remembered in a similar way. Associate them with something. If a person called Ron is tall, they are 'Long Ron'. If they seem untrustworthy they are 'Ron the Con'. And so on. It doesn't matter how ridiculous it is, as long as you remember it. The more ridiculous the better, in fact. Then reinforce the memory by taking some time to go over it mentally, for example after you have been introduced to somebody.

There are many techniques to train memory, but association is the most powerful.

77

Accept 'the full catastrophe'

JON KABAT-ZINN runs a stress-reduction clinic at the University of Massachusetts Medical Centre. In *Full Catastrophe Living* he explained what gave him the idea for the title of his book:

> I keep coming back to one line from the movie of Nikos Kazantzakis's novel *Zorba the Greek*. Zorba's young companion turns to him at a certain point and inquires, 'Zorba, have you ever been married?' to which Zorba replies (paraphrasing somewhat) 'Am I not a man? Of course I have been married. Wife, house, kids, everything... *the full catastrophe!*'

The people who came to Kabat-Zinn's clinic were finding that everyday problems – traffic, children's manners, supermarket queues – were stressing them to the point of fury. These people wished to be in control but were not. They were unable to live in the sheer mess of life. They wished everything to be perfect and ironed out, and were unable to accept life as a catastrophe, as just one damned thing after another.

What Kabat-Zinn tried to do in his book was to point out that
this random mess of life need not be considered negatively.
Inspired by the rambunctious figure of Zorba, and taking Zorba's
notion of a vital, full-spirited 'catastrophe' as his guide, Kabat-Zinn
tried to develop a view in which the 'catastrophe' of life is not an
unmitigated disaster, but a whole in which pain is mingled with
pleasure, hope with despair, joy with suffering, fear with
confidence, and illness with health. In the Kabat-Zinnian
worldview, recognizing the uncontrollable, variegated fluctuations
of existence makes it more possible to enjoy the richness of life.

78

Write the first sentence of a novel

THIS MIGHT SOUND LIKE a pointless activity, but there is a reason for doing it. It's this: you might win the Bulwer–Lytton prize for the first sentence of a novel.

The Bulwer–Lytton Prize was started in 1983 and is named after Edward George Bulwer–Lytton, whose novel *Paul Clifford* (1830) begins in the following way:

> It was a dark and stormy night; the rain fell in torrents – except at occasional intervals, when it was checked by a violent gust of wind which swept up the streets (for it is in London that our scene lies), rattling along the housetops, and fiercely agitating the scanty flame of the lamps that struggled against the darkness.

This was felt by the competition organizers to be such an absurdly prosy opening that they decided that a prize for similar efforts should be instituted. Under the rules only one sentence is allowed: the rest of the novel is not required.

A recent winner was Janice Estey, whose entry ran:

'Ace, watch your head!' hissed Wanda urgently, yet somehow provocatively, through red, full, sensuous lips, but he couldn't, you know, since nobody can actually watch more than part of his nose or a little cheek or lips if he really tries, but he appreciated her warning.

You can apply by post or online, and it's free to enter.

79

Cherish solitude (Sister Wendy does)

SISTER WENDY BECKETT lives in a trailer at a Carmelite nunnery in Norfolk. She spends most of her time in prayer, setting aside only a couple of hours for work and correspondence, and sees only the nun who brings her food and takes her laundry. She has lived in that way since 1970, emerging only to make the occasional television series. Asked once if she regretted her choice of the solitary life, she said 'Regret it? I take it that is a rhetorical question.'

Sister Wendy cherishes solitude because it allows her to become closer to God, but solitude is also valuable to non-Carmelites. If society consists of the exchange of energy from one person to another, then solitude consists of the drawing back in of energy, where it may be conserved and the mind/spirit refreshed. In the silence of solitude, whispers may be heard that are otherwise drowned out. It may be wise to heed whispers.

In the silence of solitude, whispers may be heard that are otherwise drowned out.

Solitude is not the same thing as loneliness. A person can be lonely in a crowd. In fact Byron said that it is in solitude that we are least alone.

Send out a telegram that you are not to be disturbed – hire trumpeters if necessary, or an orchestra. Slice your name from the phone book and eat the slice.

80

Get your friends to sponsor you to go to Spain and celebrate La Tomatina

A WAR WITH no winners, no losers and no casualities. This is one description of *La Tomatina*, the annual tomato-throwing festival held at Buñol, near Valencia, Spain. There is only one rule of *La Tomatina*: when in Buñol on the last Wednesday of August, throw tomatoes. The streets become a pitched battle in which everyone, old and young, male and female, is pelted with large, ripe Spanish tomatoes and soaked to their underwear in tomato juice. It is the high-point of a week-long festival with music, dancing, fireworks and heavy consumption of the local tomato-based spirit, *El Tomatorro*.

The origins of the festival are lost to history, but among the many competing theories perhaps the most probable is that it originated from a conflict between local political factions: now it has mellowed out into something resembling a town-sized frat-hall food-fight.

You can go to La Tomatina by raising money for charity. It makes a change from sky-diving or fun-running, people will be much more interested and give you more money, and you will have a lot of fun.

81

Embarrass your children / teenagers

FOR THE PURPOSES of this entry I am assuming you are not a child or teenager.

Any parent will tell you that there comes a time when their children begin to be embarrassed by their parents' behaviour. They look at their parents dancing or pulling faces, and say, with expressions of distaste: 'Dad/Mum, don't do that.'

Well, the advice of this book is *do* do that. Do it more, in fact. Become more embarrassing. Act more stupidly. It is your right to act like an idiot. Don't hold yourself back – it's bad for you. In the end your kids will admire you for it.

Children and (especially) teenagers like to trade on their effortless cool, making their elders feel they are over the hill.

Fight back, is this book's advice.

A friend of mine likes to draw up outside school gates where teenagers are kissing and blast his horn. The couples spring apart with looks of panic on their faces. He laughs uproariously as his own children scuttle out of school and get in the car. Then he drives off in a cloud of black smoke. And his kids say: 'Dad, don't do that!'

82

Work a room

INSTEAD OF GOING to parties and just talking to the people you know or are introduced to, how about using the party as a networking opportunity?

After all, it is quite possible you could hear an astounding new idea from one of the guests, fall in love with another, go on holiday to Venezuela with a third, etc. But none of this will ever happen unless you talk to them.

So you need to do some work. Try using the 'dance card' technique. Pretend you are in a Jane Austen novel and you have a card on which each of your upcoming dances is marked. Instead of dances, however, the marks are for conversations. Choose around five strangers to go on the card, and make it your business to talk to all of them. Pursue those conversations single-mindedly.

are in a Jane Austen novel.

Here's a good conversation-opener. Say simply: 'Hi, I'm Kevin,' (or your actual name), smile, and hold out your hand. This is really all that is required. You can then follow it up with a half-humorous comment such as: 'I had you down as a scientist of some kind.' This opener will give them an opportunity to say whatever it is that they actually do for a living – which you can then immediately confirm is at least as exciting as being a scientist – and the conversation is off and running.

83

Confront people politely

LET'S TAKE A COMMON situation in which you might need to confront someone politely. Some people don't clean up after their dogs. This is a health hazard. However, confronting people who let their dogs foul public spaces is not the easiest of things to do. The type of people who let their dogs evacuate wherever they will are not always the easiest type of people to deal with. That is why you have to go very gently.

Try the 'compliment' approach. 'That's a great dog,' you tell them, at some point after the dog has finished. 'Nice-looking fellow' (pat, pat), 'I wonder if I could just mention something – I saw that s/he left something behind back there. I'm not getting on your case, it's just that my children often come down here,' (or 'I often come down here', or 'my grandchildren often come down here') 'and they sometimes step in it. I just thought I'd tell you.'

This softly-softly approach is less likely to get you beaten up, and it may produce a positive response.

The key to confronting people is to be open, unthreatening, and gently assertive. If you are met with resistance, simply say: 'I'm only telling you what I think,' and walk away. You've made your point clear; next time, or the time after that, your softly-spoken words may find fertile ground.

84

Learn a trick

A 'trick' does not have to be a 'magic' trick. By 'trick' I mean any brief, astonishing performance.

It might be a conventional card trick or other magic trick. It could be a party piece such as juggling eggs, guessing the number someone is thinking of, impersonating farm animals, swallowing a cucumber, or bending a cigarette without breaking it. It could be a standing back-flip.

To have an amazing trick that you can do supremely well is to be a hero at any social gathering where people are drunk.

85

Be a representative of your country, in your country

FOR THIS TO WORK, you don't need to become an Olympic sportsperson or an ambassador. You simply need to be yourself. The idea is that when you encounter people who are visiting from different countries, you make it your business to act as a 'host' and look after them.

Tourists from countries such as the UK or USA will often be amazed at the lengths people go to in other countries to show hospitality. 'Here, share my meal.' 'Here, sleep in my bed,' etc. Exaggerations, but not by much. Which must make it pretty perplexing for these hospitable people when they come over here. No-one to welcome them. . . no-one to show them around. . . no-one to share anything. One can't help but feel that, to them, we must seem a rather stingy lot.

The remedy is surely to regard yourself as a representative of your own country and make it your business to see that people visiting, strangers who are slightly at sea in the culture that you are so familiar with, feel at home and feel welcome. Greet them. Welcome them. Be ready with tourist information. Offer to show them around – yes, actually go with them in your own time and show them things in your town. Do it for no other reason than it was done to you when you went abroad.

The remedy is surely to regard yourself as a representative of your own country and make it your business to see that people visiting feel at home and feel welcome.

86

Try lucid dreaming

LUCID DREAMING DIFFERS from ordinary dreaming in that the dreamer is aware that he or she is dreaming, and can control the things that happen in the dream.

If this sounds impossible, a few simple techniques will help.

First, become more aware of your dreaming generally. Keep a journal to record your dreams.

Second, have a 'dream-goal' in mind before you go to sleep. Decide, for example, that you want to dream about flying. You could write a journal entry describing what you want to do.

Third, notice when you most commonly have dreams. The period just after falling asleep is an easy time to become lucid, because there is a 'twilight zone' that mingles conscious and dreaming thoughts. With practice, you may be able to prolong this period. Setting an alarm to 'snooze' and deliberately and repeatedly falling back asleep can do it. Many people find that afternoon naps are the best time to lucid dream.

Finally, try to set an 'awareness trigger'. This is an action that you deliberately repeat during the day, such as counting on your fingers. If you do it so often that it becomes habitual, it will carry over into your dream, but in the dream you will find that there is some divergence from the normal waking experience: you will have 11 fingers, or some will be blurred, etc. Then you will realize you are dreaming, and the dream will become lucid.

87

Come to terms with ageing

WE ALL DREAD our birthdays after the age of 21 and want to stay young forever. But fear of ageing is a terribly negative and destructive thing. It diminishes one's enjoyment of life and fosters feelings of inadequacy and exclusion. It's also what they call in Japan a 'luxury problem': that is, it's only a problem if you have the luxury to perceive it as a problem. For much of the world you're very lucky if you live to be old. Only the fortunate grow up to have arthritis. The others are dead before they get there.

Here are some thoughts that might help you come to terms with ageing. First, no-one is guaranteed tomorrow. Old and young are in the same boat, poised on the edge of extinction, and in relation to death, we are all the same age. Second, happiness is the prerogative of no age, and anyone who tells you otherwise is misleading you or works in advertising; there are plenty of miserable teenagers. Third, if you are granted any sort of life you have an opportunity to do something with it; if you are granted a long life then you have extra time to get it done. Fourth, the infirmities of age, while real, are part of the human condition, and to grow old is to participate in humanity's common lot. Age allows you to understand and become closer to your parents, grandparents, and their parents and grandparents. To be young forever would be to be crippled.

88

Be a bookcrosser

BOOKCROSSING IS THE WORLD'S biggest free book club, with three-quarters of a million members in around 130 countries. There are no membership subscriptions, nothing is ever sent in the post, and there is no obligation ever to buy anything. The idea instead is to share your books with people by leaving them in public places: on park benches, in tea-houses, on the bus, on church pews or in changing rooms.

Each book is first registered online so it can be individually tagged as a Bookcrossing book. Members write the Bookcrossing ID number of the book inside it and release it into the wild. The person who picks it up can (if they wish) log on to the Bookcrossing site to say they've found it, before themselves re-releasing it (after reading it, obviously). In this way a Bookcrossing book can travel around the world, its former owners following its journey like anxious parents keeping tabs on a gap-year child.

Bookcrossing is worthwhile for several reasons: it clears your bookshelves of books that you've enjoyed but would like to pass on; it brings you into contact with an online community of readers where books are discussed, reviewed, rated and tracked; and it's possible to hunt for books that have recently been released in your area. To date, nearly six million books have been registered, and it's quite likely there are dozens floating around near you. In effect it makes the world one big free library.

It makes the world one big free library.

89

Teach a child something fun

CHILDREN NEED TO BE taught things. Why not be the one that teaches them? If you do it sweetly and considerately, they'll always remember it.

For example, children need to know how to:

Ride a bike
Swim
Make scrambled eggs
Do a simple card trick
Play cat's cradle
Play with a yo-yo
Produce a penny from behind someone's ear
Name the stars and constellations

. . . and many more things. This is usually the province of the parents, but if they are too busy or have been otherwise derelict in their duty, and if you are lucky enough to be an uncle, aunt, neighbour or guardian, those newly-developing and information-hungry young minds are yours for the teaching. (Just don't 'teach' them about God or politics, because if you do the parents probably won't let you within a million miles of them ever again.)

90

Make your gratitude less perfunctory

ACCORDING TO A RECENT book about the life of a supermarket till attendant, *Checkout*, supermarket customers are very annoying. They are unhygienic (they sneeze on you), ill-prepared, witless, prone to anger, need simple things to be explained over and over again, but most trying of all, they are *rude*. They start loud mobile phone conversations rather than say hello, and generally treat the till attendant as if she/he is some sort of amoeba.

Why do we treat public servants so badly? Maybe it's time to reconsider our attitude towards people who do things for us. A good start might be to thank people we would not normally thank. A postman or postwoman is an obvious example. If they deliver you a bulky parcel that they've been schlepping around with them on their rounds all day, some special recognition is called for when they ring your bell because it won't fit through the letterbox. Tell them you can see it must have been heavy, that you appreciate them carrying it around, and give them a smile. Or if you are in a shoe shop and have tried on several pairs of shoes without buying anything, tell the assistant you really appreciate their patience.

One might argue that these people are being paid to do their job and that therefore no extra thanks are called for. But if they had been surly it would have had a bad impact on your day – and yet it would not have contravened their job description.

If anyone has done something with care and expertise, why shouldn't you thank them warmly?

91

Give away your superfluous possessions

WHEN YOU DEPART this life, someone is going to have to sift through all your junk and get rid of it – and some of it is going to be very embarrassing. Why not do them and yourself a favour and get rid of it now? That way, when your time comes, you will leave this world with tasteful minimalism.

Someone else might be able to use your junk anyway: your unwanted rabbit hutch, your old children's bikes, the books you haven't read for decades and never will, and all the other superfluous objects that you have been keeping in storage for so long they've gathered a thick layer of dust. To dispose of them will rid you of the nagging feeling of guilt you have every time you look at them, and the fear that one day your junk will rise up and overwhelm you.

A good option is to join a scheme such as Freecycle, which matches people to superfluous possessions. You don't need to pay for a skip, and your eager contacts will come and take it away.

92

Grow huge sunflowers

SUNFLOWERS ARE ASTONISHING plants. They grow astoundingly fast, especially if you give them a good start in some nice compost, protect them from pests, and water and feed them regularly. A mature sunflower can grow up to three metres high, and its flower-head can block out the sun itself. Even the dead stalks are curiously impressive – they rustle against one another in winter. And you can eat the seeds.

A personal experience: I grow sunflowers every year in my front garden. Last year a young woman I had never met called at my door and asked if she could have one of my sunflowers to cast in bronze. She did so and sent me a photograph.

93

Smile

YOU MAY REMEMBER occasions in your life, perhaps many years ago, when people you didn't know smiled at you, seemingly for no reason. The reason you still remember it is because it made you feel so good.

A smile sends a message that the other person (the smilee) is worthy of notice, that the smiler is affably disposed towards them. To receive such a message from a stranger, for no apparent reason, is quite shocking.

If you smile at

In the field of your ordinary social life, try observing people's reactions when you give them your most open, frank and beaming smile, directed at them while you look them in the eye. It really hits them. They become more receptive, more friendly (and more easy to manipulate, but that's another story). Sometimes a heartfelt smile can lift someone's spirits to such an extent that they treat you differently forever after.

If you smile at people they tend to smile back. You can do this as you walk down the street. In fact, you can set yourself the challenge of seeing how many smiles you can elicit as you walk. Just smile at them – no need to tell jokes or juggle. You can even say 'Nice Day.' They won't write you into their will, but they are unlikely to forget it in a hurry.

people they tend to smile back.

94

Go bell-ringing

BELL-RINGING IS AN ANCIENT ART practised worldwide. Bells are rung in churches for weddings, celebrations and funerals but also just for pleasure. Anyone can do it with a little instruction and practice. Beginners often start on handbells before progressing on to church bells.

Those who do it say they have made friends (sometimes all over the world), got fit, and improved their maths. There are so many permutations to the 'changes' that can be rung on a set of church bells that bell-ringing becomes a lifelong learning experience; professional mathematicians have even investigated bell-ringing changes in terms of the branch of mathematics known as group theory.

Strangely enough it's now possible to take part in bell-ringing at home. A home-based bell-ringing simulator can be mounted in a loft or upper room, with the traditional 'sally' (hand-rope) dangling from it: it is then plugged into a computer or laptop which helps the ringer to replicate the various changes.

95

Form a debating club

HERE'S A MORAL dilemma. Your neighbour has been caught shoplifting on CCTV. The police have identified him and know where he lives, but he's never at home. They ask you to keep an eye out for him and call them if he returns. Do you co-operate? Obviously you would if it were something really bad, but shoplifting?

This is one example of a minor moral dilemma. Other moral dilemmas might involve questions involving religion, sex or politics. Do religious beliefs ever justify breaking the law? Why is adultery legal in some countries but illegal in others? What about abortion – is it morally wrong or not, and in what circumstances?

One might go through the whole gamut of moral issues and try to crystallize one's own view. What would one do in any particular situation? What is your code of conduct?

Form a debating club with a few friends. Convene in a pub or café. Really thrash things out. Discussion encourages critical thinking and promotes tolerance for the opinions of others. And in a democracy, it's free.

96

Take your shoes off and walk in the dew on a sunny morning

In summer, dew falls early and lingers on into the morning. Sun strikes the clipped grass of lawns and parks, but does not have the strength to bake it dry; the dew warms up and hangs in drops on the tips and edges of each green spear. There the drops wait, balanced, perfect, a million liquid jewels in a tiny jungle, each jewel at blood temperature. Even late in the morning in summer there are still patches of dew in shadowy places; only by noon does the earth exhale its last moist breath.

To lay waste to these fields of diamonds with a pair of shoes would be a desecration. So take off your shoes. Now walk. Feel as the wet bathes your feet, balloons of dew exploding on your heels, instep and toes.

What a mysterious gift! How magnificently unnecessary!

In Poland they appreciate the dew. The Polish for 'dew' is 'rosa', and it is a name often given to girls.

Feel as the
wet bathes your feet,
balloons of dew exploding
on your heels, instep
and toes.

97

Dress up

ONE DAY A WEEK, put aside your usual clothes and do something out of the ordinary.

If you work in a hairdresser's, discard the designer jeans and T-shirt, and turn up wearing a business suit.

If you work on a building site, turn up wearing a sarong and love-beads.

If you work as an architect, turn up dressed as a tramp.

If you only do this one day a week no-one will have the energy to complain. They'll even look forward to whatever you come up with next. 'Dress-up Mondays' will become a by-word for weird and kooky excess.

At the hairdresser's, clients will praise your fashion sense.

At the building site, colleagues will admit their secret desires to do the same.

At the architect's, clients will be stunned by your chutzpah.

If clothes make a statement, then one day a week why not make it a statement worth hearing?

98

Give up your TV

THIS NEED NOT BE as drastic as it sounds. You don't need to give up watching TV – you just need to give up paying for it.

In many countries – the UK for example – you have to pay to watch TV. You buy a licence every year and that entitles you to watch. But new technology is making that an increasingly unworkable model. In the UK, most of the BBC's programmes, as well as those of the other channels (which technically are not paid for by the licence but by advertising) are available to view online without purchasing a licence (except 'live' broadcasts such as news). After you have unhooked your TV aerial, the programming is essentially free. And legal.

But not everyone wants to watch TV on their computer. The solution is to rig your computer up to your TV. You can do this either with a wireless router or with a cable. In both cases the money you save on the licence will easily cover the cost. If you want to go one step better, try it with a Nintendo Wii and some Opera software. That way your computer doesn't even need to be turned on to access the programming.

Unhooking yourself from your aerial (and your licence) means that you will probably watch less TV: you won't channel-surf, and will plan your viewing, watching only the shows that really interest you.

99

Be 'Lord' for a day

THIS IS A GAME that you can play with a few friends while on holiday, or when spending any extended period of time together.

Each person takes it in turn to be 'Lord' for the day. This means that the others must address him or her as 'my Lord' or 'my Lady' and do whatever they ask (within reason and the law of the land). The 'Lord' makes all the decisions about where to go, what to do, what to eat, etc., and has any task performed for him immediately – with no carping or debate. Then the next day the next person takes over and they become 'Lord'.

Unless you have played this game it is difficult to imagine how liberating it is. Suddenly all the typical arguments and negotiations over what should be done disappear – which saves a lot of time. The burden of responsibility is lifted from the Lord's 'subjects', they have to do things which they would never normally do, and may end up being pleasantly surprised at how much they enjoy them. And everyone gets a turn to make the decisions (and mistakes) and be waited on hand and foot.

Different 'Lords' have different styles. Some are draconian; others are benign; others, unused to absolute power, remain indecisive; still others are keen to exact revenge. As an experiment in practical psychology, it can't be beaten.

100

Write fewer emails and more letters

AS MENTIONED on page 126, emails have severe deficiencies when it comes to the expression of anything important. They are soulless. There is none of the personality of handwriting, no cream laid paper, no watermark, no stamps, no postmarks, no letterhead, no flowing signature.

Letters are nice things to receive and nice things to keep. A letter or postcard coming through the door will always be more welcome than an email or e-card. What sort of person sends birthday e-cards anyway?

Emails may not even be the best option for general enquiries or business correspondence. These days, when fewer and fewer people send letters, a communication by post can elicit a much more considered response. It's fantastic for complaints, for example. A nicely-written letter of complaint to a utility company, online clothing store, etc., will be taken more seriously than an email, and may get you a better result. Members of Parliament will respond more fully and carefully to a letter than to an email.

Letters provide a sense of occasion, almost of drama. They warm the heart. A letter can make a difference that an email cannot. Why not write to someone who needs a letter? A lonely person on Valentine's Day? Someone in prison? A friend you haven't seen for a while?

IOI

Don't expect that things will be different in Tenerife

ALAIN DE BOTTON warns in his book *The Art of Travel* that we go on holiday at our peril. Far from 'getting away from it all', we are liable to take all our problems with us and spend the time worrying about our work or arguing with our spouses and children. 'I think resorts should offer discreet temples to disappointment,' de Botton says, 'where travellers could break off from their couple and, for a few moments, confess the scale of their disappointment and anger to a sympathetic priestly type, before heading back to the beach.' According to a poll in a 2009 issue of *Glamour* magazine, a third of all couples start rowing by the second day of their holiday.

This might lead you to consider the following: why do you need to go on holiday? What is wrong with your life right now? Why do you need, in fact, to spend a great deal of money doing something that will bring you doubtful enjoyment, that you will need a holiday to recover from, and from which you will return to work with a surge of gratitude? The time to be at one with ourselves, discover and accept who we are, is right now, not on holiday. If doing that is too difficult, then it won't be any easier in Tenerife.

102

Find out what's happening near you and join in

NEAR YOU AT THE MOMENT are very probably the following things: a local radio station, a historical society, a school, a women's institute, a theatre group, a writer's circle, a rugby club, an adult education centre, a village hall, a book club, a music ensemble, a rambler's club, a cycling club, a historical re-enactment society, various campaigning groups, preservation societies, political parties. . . and much more. Most of them will be free to join (or require a small subscription), and the people you will meet and the things you will do will take your life in strange and unpredictable directions.

One of the secrets of a happy life must surely be this: the realization that people are more important than things. The more people you meet, the better are your chances of forming friendships and relationships that will enrich your life. And beyond that, simply to do something – perhaps something you're a little scared of – is a source of great power (see page 62). It might be delivering meals on wheels (see page 102), starting a film society (see page 38), joining a gardening scheme (see page 140) or running a restaurant from your living-room (see page 36). Whatever it is, join in!

Suggested Reading and Resources

Athill, Diana: *Somewhere Towards the End* (Granta, 2008)
De Botton, Alain: *The Art of Travel* (Pantheon, 2002)
Edwards, Betty: *Drawing on the Right Side of the Brain*
    (Fontana, 1983)
Hill, Jason: *Wild Foods of Britain* (Adam & Charles Black, 1939)
Kabat-Zinn, Jon: *Full Catastrophe Living* (Piatkus, 1990)
Jeffers, Susan: *Feel the Fear and Do It Anyway* (Arrow, 1991)
Keene, Donald: *Essays in Idleness* (ed. of the Tsurezuregusa of Kenkou)
    (Columbia, 1967)
Larkin, Philip: *The Whitsun Weddings* (Faber, 1964)
Lewis-Stempel, John: *The Wild Life* (Doubleday, 2009)
Lewycka, Marina: *We Are All Made of Glue* (Fig Tree, 2009)
Lindsay, Vachel: *The Congo and Other Poems* (Dodo Press, 2009)
Mabey, Richard: *Food for Free* (Collins Gem, 2004)
Moran, Michael: *Sod Abroad* (John Murray, 2008)
Orwell, George: *Nineteen Eighty-Four* (Secker & Warburg, 1949)
Peterson, B.R.: *The Original Roadkill Cookbook, or Yellow Line
Yummies* (Ten Speed Press, 1988)
Sam, Anna: *Checkout: A Life on the Tills* (Gallic Press, 2009)
Vonnegut, Kurt: *Breakfast of Champions* (Delacorte Press, 1973)
Weeks, David: *Eccentrics: A Study of Sanity and Strangeness*
    (Random House, 1995)

The Bulwer-Lytton Fiction Contest:
http://www.bulwer-lytton.com

Freecycle UK:
http://www.uk.freecycle.org

Guinness Book of Records applications:
http://www.guinnessworldrecords.com/register/login.aspx

Project Gutenberg:
http://www.gutenberg.org/wiki/Main_Page